W0404190

Willy Hailer Anton Ritzer

PFAFFENHOFEN

AN DER ILM

Ein zweisprachiges Portrait der l(i)ebenswerten Kreisstadt
im Hopfenland Hallertau

A bilingual portrait of this liveable and loveable city
in the hop-growing region of Hallertau

Edition Galli Verlag

INHALT
CONTENTS

PFAFFENHOFEN A. D. ILM
Guter Boden für große Vorhaben

1

EDITORIAL
FOREWORD

15 Jahre nach Erscheinen unseres ersten gemeinsamen Pfaffenhofen-Buches sind wir gerne der Bitte von Verleger Josef Galli gefolgt, an einem neuen Bildband mitzuwirken. So waren wir in den vergangenen Monaten unterwegs, um unsere schöne Heimatstadt mit der Kamera neu zu entdecken.

Nicht selten war unser Blick durch den Sucher von Wehmut getrübt. Denn so manche vertraute Gebäude und idyllische Winkel, die uns als Fotomotive in den vergangenen Jahrzehnten wie gute Freunde begleitet hatten, sind mittlerweile für immer verschwunden. Und draußen in den Dörfern werden die Landschaft und das gewachsene Ortsbild zunehmend von Solardächern verschandelt.

Bei allem nostalgischen Bedauern überwiegt aber doch der positive Eindruck, dass sich in unserer schönen Heimatstadt sehr Vieles zum Besseren verändert hat. Zum Beispiel die Neugestaltung des Hauptplatzes, die Belebung des Handels, der Straßengastronomie und vor allem auch des kulturellen Angebotes. Eindrucksvolle Bestätigung für diese positive Entwicklung ist die Auszeichnung als „lebenswerteste Stadt" beim LivCom-Award 2011.

Das Ergebnis unserer jetzt vorliegenden Arbeit verstehen wir als eine fotografische Liebeserklärung an unsere Heimatstadt. In über 260 Bildern präsentieren wir Pfaffenhofen als lebens- und liebenswerte Kommune mit florierender Wirtschaft, hochkarätigem Kulturangebot, vielfältigen Sport- und Freizeiteinrichtungen, Naturschönheiten und historischen Sehenswürdigkeiten. Die Fotos zeigen Gebäude, Straßen, Plätze und Landschaften auch aus ungewohnten Perspektiven, die dem Betrachter einen neuen Blick auf vertraute Ansichten eröffnen und dazu mahnen sollen, mit dem schützenswerten baulichen Erbe und der Natur achtsam umzugehen.

Auch die Pfaffenhofener Ortsteile sowie einige Sehenswürdigkeiten im Landkreis Pfaffenhofen werden in dem Bildband vorgestellt. So soll unser Buch sowohl alteingesessene Pfaffenhofener als auch Neubürger, Touristen und Geschäftsreisende zur fotografischen Entdekkungsreise durch die Stadt und deren Umland einladen.

Willy Hailer *Anton Ritzer*

Fifteen years after our first joint book on Pfaffenhofen was published, we were happy to comply with a request from the publisher Josef Galli to work with him on a new illustrated book on the city. Which is why we've been travelling these past few months, rediscovering our beautiful home city and capturing it all on camera.

Not infrequently, the scene through our viewfinder was clouded by a feeling of wistfulness, for many of the familiar buildings and idyllic little nooks that in past decades had served as photo motifs and accompanied us like good friends have disappeared for ever. And out in the countryside, the landscape and overall appearance of villages that have evolved over time are being increasingly disfigured by solar roofs.

And yet, in spite of all the nostalgic regret, the prevailing mood is a positive one, that a great many of the changes in our delightful city have been for the best. Take, for example, the redesign of its main square, the revitalization of trade, the street cafés and outdoor eateries, and above all, its cultural attractions – positive developments that were impressively confirmed when the city was honoured with title of "Most Liveable City" at the 2011 LivCom Awards.

We look upon the results of our present work as a photographic declaration of love to our home city. In more than 260 pictures, we show Pfaffenhofen as a liveable and loveable community with a flourishing economy, top-class cultural activities, a wide range of sporting and leisure facilities, scenic attractions and places of historical interest. Some of the buildings, streets, squares and landscapes are shown from unusual perspectives to open up new views of otherwise familiar sights. They are also intended to remind those viewing them to treat nature with care and to be respectful towards those parts of our architectural heritage that have been identified as worthy of protection.

By introducing the reader to the various parts of the city and to several points of interest in the Pfaffenhofen administrative district, we hope this illustrated book will serve as an invitation to long-time residents and new inhabitants, tourists and business travellers alike to embark on a photographic voyage of discovery through the city and its surrounding areas.

Willy Hailer *Anton Ritzer*

2

ZUM GELEIT
PREFACE

Wir leben in einer schönen Stadt! Wie schön sie wirklich ist, das wird uns beim Blättern in dem neuen Bildband von Willy Hailer und Anton Ritzer wieder so richtig bewusst. Mit wunderbaren Aufnahmen führen uns die beiden Fotografen die Attraktivität und Vielseitigkeit unserer Heimat vor Augen. „Fotografieren heißt Bedeutung verleihen“, hat die amerikanische Schriftstellerin Susan Sontag einmal gesagt. Die Autoren des vorliegenden Bildbands haben viele Motive fotografiert, die für uns von Bedeutung sind. Sie haben aber auch manche Details, neue Sichtweisen und ungewohnte Blickwinkel entdeckt, die uns im Alltag oft verborgen bleiben und die jetzt eine neue Bedeutung erhalten. So lernen wir unsere Stadt und ihre Umgebung wieder ein Stückchen neu kennen und sehen so manches Gebäude, so manche Straße mit anderen Augen.

Mit ihrem Buch dokumentieren Willy Hailer und Anton Ritzer auch die Veränderungen, die es in den vergangenen 15 Jahren in unserer Stadt gegeben hat, und machen es damit auch zu einem interessanten Nachschlagewerk für kommende Generationen. Dabei haben sie ihre persönlichen Akzente gesetzt, gehen auch auf negative Entwicklungen ein, zeigen uns aber vor allem, wie liebenswert unsere Heimat ist und was ihren Lebenswert ausmacht.

So ist der neue Bildband eine Hommage an Pfaffenhofen geworden und eine schöne Möglichkeit, allen Besuchern von außerhalb sowie auch den Neubürgern unsere Stadt zu präsentieren. Sehr hilfreich ist dabei, dass der gesamte Text des Buches in Deutsch und Englisch abgedruckt ist, um unsere „lebenswerteste Stadt der Welt“ auch den vielen ausländischen Gästen und internationalen Geschäftspartnern der örtlichen Unternehmen nahe zu bringen.

Die Erarbeitung des Bildbandes war eine umfangreiche Aufgabe, der sich die beiden Autoren mit viel Engagement und Herzblut gestellt haben. Ich darf ihnen, ebenso wie dem Galli-Verlag, im Namen der Stadt Pfaffenhofen herzlich für dieses Werk danken! Ich wünsche dem Buch viel Erfolg und zahlreiche interessierte Leser. Allen, die in dem Buch blättern, wünsche ich viel Freude beim Betrachten der Bilder und viele interessante Einblicke.

Herzlich Ihr
Thomas Herker 1. Bürgermeister der Stadt Pfaffenhofen a. d. Ilm

We live in a beautiful city. Just how beautiful it really is becomes clear as we leaf through the many wonderful pictures in this new book highlighting the appeal and diversity of our home city by the photographers Willy Hailer and Anton Ritzer. American author Susan Sontag once said that to photograph is to confer meaning. The authors of this illustrated book have photographed many motifs that mean a great deal to us. But they've also discovered a number of details, unusual perspectives and fresh views of things that often remain hidden to us, but which now take on a new significance. This in turn gives us an opportunity to rediscover our city and its surroundings and to see some of its buildings and streets with different eyes.

With their photographs, Willy Hailer and Anton Ritzer have, in addition, documented the changes the city has undergone in the past 15 years, which will make the book an interesting work of reference for coming generations. In the process, they have also added their own personal touches, addressing negative trends as well positive ones, but all the while focusing on how loveable our home is and what it is that makes life here so worthwhile.

And so this new book of photographs has become both an hommage to Pfaffenhofen and an ideal opportunity to present the city not only to its visitors, but also to those who have recently settled here. The fact that the entire text of the book has been published in English as well German will even help to bring our "most loveable city in the world" closer to foreign guests and the international business partners of local companies.

Compiling this illustrated book was an enormous challenge and both authors faced up to it with a great deal of dedication and lifeblood. On behalf of the city of Pfaffenhofen, I should like to offer Willy Hailer and Anton Ritzer, as well as the publishers, Galli Verlag, our warmest thanks. May the book be greatly successful and find many, many interested readers. And to all those who turn its pages to view the pictures, I wish you much pleasure and many interesting insights.

Sincerely yours,
Thomas Herker Mayor of the City of Pfaffenhofen an der Ilm

Die älteste Darstellung von Pfaffenhofen schuf der Hofmaler Hans Donauer um das Jahr 1590 als eines von zahlreichen Deckenfresken bayerischer Ortsansichten im Antiquarium der Münchener Residenz. Aus Richtung Süden betrachtet, ist die um 1430 fertig gestellte Stadtmauer mit dem heute noch erhaltenen Hungerturm (rechts) zu erkennen.
The oldest-known depiction of Pfaffenhofen was created by the court painter Hans Donauer around 1590 as one of many ceiling frescos of Bavarian townscapes in the Antiquarium of the Munich Residence. Viewed here from the south, one can see the city wall, completed around 1430, with the medieval jail known as the *Hungerturm* (far right), which still exists today.

3 DIE HISTORISCHEN WURZELN
THE HISTORICAL ROOTS

Von der Steinzeitsiedlung zur lebendigen Kreisstadt

Pfaffenhofen war schon vor 6500 Jahren besiedelt

Das Gebiet in der Umgebung der Kreisstadt vor etwa zwei bis 60 Millionen Jahren: Durch die Verschiebung des afrikanischen Kontinents nach Norden und die Hebung der eurasischen Festlandplatte werden in der Tertiärzeit die Alpen aufgefaltet. Nördlich des Gebirges sind weite Teile des Landes noch von Seitenarmen des Ur-Meeres Thethys bedeckt. Nach dem Rückzug der Wassermassen bleiben mächtige Sedimentschichten zurück, deren versteinerte Überreste heute die Landschaft im fränkischen Jura prägen. Während der folgenden Eiszeiten breiten sich die Gletscher von den Bergen weit nach Norden ins Alpenvorland aus. Perioden extremer Kälte werden immer wieder unterbrochen von wärmeren Phasen, in denen die Schmelzwasserfluten über weit verzweigte Flusssysteme riesige Geröllmassen, Ton- und Sandschichten aus der Molasse des Hochgebirges auch in unsere Gegend transportie-

From stone age settlement to vibrant district capital

Pfaffenhofen was already inhabited 6,500 years ago

It's the Tertiary Period, between two and 60 million years ago – and the region in question is the area surrounding what is today Pfaffenhofen, the district capital: the northward shift of the African continent and the lifting of the Eurasian Plate has led to the creation of the Alps. To the north of the mountains, wide regions of the country are still submerged under the side arms of a primal ocean. The masses of water recede, leaving behind mighty sedimentary layers. In the various ice ages that follow, glaciers spread from the mountains far north to the pre-Alpine foothills. Subsequent periods of extreme cold are repeatedly interspersed by warmer phases, during which the meltwater floods also transport giant masses of scree and layers of clay and sand – from the molasse of the high mountain range via widely branched river systems – to our region, where they form the typical Tertiary hilly landscape.

Grabungsleiter Markus Arnolds und sein Kollege Bernd Kriens begutachten mit Alfred Zeitler und Investor Hans Baierl von Trend-Immobilien (von links) die historischen Funde auf dem Bortenschlager-Areal.

Excavation leader Markus Arnolds and his colleague Bernd Kriens examine historic finds at the Bortenschlager site with Alfred Zeitler and investor Hans Baierl from Trend-Immobilien (from left to right).

ren und auf diese Weise die typische tertiäre Hügellandschaft formen. Das subtropische Klima, das zwischen den Eiszeiten herrscht, bietet ideale Lebensbedingungen für große Landsäugetiere. Dass sie auch das Gebiet des heutigen Landkreises Pfaffenhofen bewohnten, belegt ein spektakulärer Fund im April 2002 in Junkenhofen bei Gerolsbach. Dort kam in einer Kiesgrube das Skelett des Urelefanten Archaeobelodon zum Vorschein, der vor etwa 15 Millionen Jahren hier gelebt hatte. Für die Fachwelt eine Sensation, denn weltweit konnten bisher nur drei Exemplare dieser Art entdeckt werden.

Erste Spuren menschlicher Existenz lassen sich in der Donauebene und im angrenzenden Jura schon aus der Altsteinzeit (vor 100 000 Jahren) nachweisen. In die lange von Sümpfen und dichtem Urwald bedeckten Landstriche weiter südlich wagen sich die Jäger und Sammler zunächst wohl nicht vor. Erst aus der Mittel- und Jungsteinzeit (8000 bis 2000 v. Chr.) gibt es dann häufigere Funde von Waffen und Werkzeugen wie Steinäxte, Speerspitzen und Faustkeile auch im Raum Pfaffenhofen. Aus den herumziehenden Jägern und Sammlern sind beim Übergang von der Mittel- zur Jungsteinzeit (etwa ab 5500 v. Chr.) bereits sesshafte Bauern geworden, die

Keramikscherben und andere Spuren aus der so genannten Münchshöfener Jungsteinzeit-Kultur wurden im Sommer 2011 bei Ausgrabungen im Stadtzentrum gefunden. Sie belegen, dass schon vor 6500 Jahren Menschen in Pfaffenhofen siedelten.

Ceramic fragments and other traces from the so-called Münchshöfen Neolithic Age culture were unearthed during excavations in the city centre in the summer of 2011. What these prove is that there was already a human settlement in Pfaffenhofen 6,500 years ago.

The subtropical climate that prevailed between the different ice ages provided the ideal living environment for large land mammals. That they also inhabited the area of the present-day Pfaffenhofen administrative district was proved by a spectacular find in April 2002, when the skeleton of an *Archaeobelodon*, a prehistoric mammoth that lived here around 15 million years ago, turned up in a gravel pit in Junkenhofen near Gerolsbach.

Evidence of the early traces of human existence dating back as far as the Palaeolithic Age (100,000 years ago) has also been found in the Danube Basin and the adjoining Jura region. At first, the hunters and gatherers probably didn't venture further south into the areas long covered by swamps and dense primeval forest. More frequent finds of weapons, including in the Pfaffenhofen area, date back to much later periods: the Mesolithic Age and the Neolithic Age (8000 to 2000 BC). In the transition from the Mesolithic to the Neolithic Age (around 5600 to 5500 BC), the migrant hunters and gatherers have become settled farmers who keep livestock and erect small rural settlements and timber-post houses.

Back in 1987, archaeologists unearthed evidence of earlier settlement activity in the area around Pfaffenhofen, on a wooded hill on the north-eastern outskirts of Eberstetten. What they initially discovered there – next to the remains of fortifications, presumably a princely residence, protected by ramparts and palisades and dating from the Hallstatt period (around 500 BC) – were considerably older fragments of pottery and traces of burnt buildings from around 1800 BC. Scientific proof that humans had already settled the Ilm Valley area near Pfaffenhofen much earlier, about 4,000 years before the birth of Christ, didn't emerge until August 2011, when archaeologists excavating at the Bortenschlager

Nutztiere halten und kleine dörfliche Siedlungen mit Pfostenhäusern errichten.

Schon 1987 fanden Archäologen erste Nachweise einer früheren Siedlungstätigkeit in der Umgebung von Pfaffenhofen auf einem bewaldeten Hügel am nordöstlichen Ortsrand von Eberstetten. Dort stießen sie zunächst auf Überreste einer mit Wällen und Palisaden gesicherten Wehranlage, vermutlich ein Fürstensitz, aus der Hallstattzeit (etwa um 500 v. Chr.). Bei weiteren Ausgrabungen kamen dann auch noch wesentlich ältere Keramikscherben und Spuren verbrannter Gebäude aus der Zeit um 1800 v. Chr. zum Vorschein. Dass aber schon wesentlich früher, rund 4000 Jahre vor Christi Geburt, Menschen das Ilmtal bei Pfaffenhofen besiedelt hatten, ist erst seit August 2011 wissenschaftlich belegt. Bei Ausgrabungen auf der Baustelle des Bortenschlager-Areals mitten im Pfaffenhofener Stadtzentrum fanden Archäologen Keramikreste mit typischer Ornamentverzierung aus der so genannten Münchshöfener Kultur, die um 4500 v. Chr. begann und etwa 700 Jahre dauerte.

Markus Arnolds, Grabungsleiter der Neuburger Firma ADV, schließt aus, dass die am Hauptplatz gefundenen Keramikfragmente von durchziehenden Jungsteinzeit-Menschen einfach weggeworfen worden oder später auf andere Weise zufällig hierher gekommen sein könnten. Der von seinem Kollegen Bernd Kriens in zwei Metern Tiefe an der Auenstraße gesicherte archäologische Befund sei eindeutig. „Hier haben Jungsteinzeit-Menschen vor über 6000 Jahren in Hütten gelebt und auch schon Ackerbau und Viehzucht betrieben", so Markus Arnolds.

Die Wissenschaft geht davon aus, dass die Besiedelung des süddeutschen Raumes in der Jungsteinzeit über Griechenland und den Balkan erfolgte. Entlang der Flusstäler zogen die Menschen nach Westen und wurden hier sesshaft. Die meisten Fundstätten dieser Epoche liegen an der Donau in Niederbayern, wie in der Ortschaft Münchshöfen (Landkreis Straubing-Bogen), der die Kultur ihren Namen verdankt.

Pfaffenhofen ist einer der wenigen oberbayerischen Orte, wo sich die Münchshöfener Steinzeitmenschen relativ weit von der Donau entfernt nachweisen lassen. Der Platz unweit des Zusammenflusses von Gerolsbach und Ilm war für die Siedler wohl sehr attraktiv. „Die Menschen brauchten Wasser für sich und das Vieh und haben deshalb auch möglichst nahe am Fluss gesiedelt", so Arnolds. Zudem hätte der nahe gelegene Höhenrücken im Westen des heutigen Hauptplatzes jederzeit Schutz bei Überschwemmungen geboten.

Markus Arnolds und Bernd Kriens halten es für sehr wahrscheinlich, dass der Ort auch später immer wieder besiedelt und somit die eigentliche Keimzelle der Stadt Pfaffenhofen war. Eine Bestätigung für diese Annahme gibt es bisher allerdings nicht. Denn die Hoffnung der Archäolo-

building site in central Pfaffenhofen found ceramic remains decorated with ornamentation typical of the so-called Münchshöfen culture, which lasted for about 700 years beginning in around 4500 BC.

Markus Arnolds, dig leader at the ADC company in Neuburg, has ruled out the possibility that the ceramic fragments found in the main square may have been left behind by Neolithic humans passing through the area, or that they could have ended up there accidentally by some other means. The significance of the archaeological artefact found two metres below ground at Auenstrasse by his colleague Bernd Kriens is unmistakable. According to Markus Arnolds: "Neolithic Age humans were living here in huts 6,000 years ago, and were already cultivating crops and raising livestock." Scientists believe the colonization of southern Germany during the Neolithic Period occurred via Greece and the Balkans, with groups migrating westwards along the river valleys to settle here. Most of the archaeological sites of discovery relating to this epoch are located on the Danube in Lower Bavaria, such as in the village of Münchshöfen (in the Straubing-Bogen administrative district), which lent its name to the culture.

Pfaffenhofen is one of the few places in Upper Bavaria in which the presence of Münchshöfen Stone Age man can be proved at such a relatively great distance from the Danube. Markus Arnolds and Bernd Kriens think it very likely that the location at which the Ilm River and Gerolsbach meet was resettled later, again and again, and thus became the actual nucleus of the city of Pfaffenhofen – a hypothesis that has yet to be proved, for at their excavation sites, archaeologists are still hoping to find traces from the time immediately preceding the first documented mention, in the 12th century, of Pfaffenhofen as a market. "Apart from the Neolithic ceramic remains, all the other finds evaluated so far date back to around 1300 or later," says dig leader Bernd Kriens. For this reason, the date and circumstances of the town's foundation remain unclear.

For many years, the most likely theory was the one advanced by Pfaffenhofen's local historian and honorary citizen Heinrich Streidl (1909–1989) and other historians, that Pfaffenhofen was founded by monks from the Benedictine monastery at Ilmmünster, which is mentioned in a 9th-century document. Near Altenstadt, today the site of the municipal cemetery and the St Andreas church, the monks are said to have set up an agricultural outpost, the Pfaffen-Höfe ("clerics' farmyards"). Later, around 1190, Bavaria's Duke Ludwig the Kelheimer (1173–1231) founded his new market and administrative centre one kilometre south of the original village of Altenstadt, on the green meadow, so to speak.

That, at least, is the popular foundation theory, albeit one that Markus Arnolds feels is no longer tenable. "We can probably assume that the city area as we know it today had already been settled long before

Die St. Andreaskirche in Altenstadt (oben rechts) und die romanische Basilika St. Arsatius in Ilmmünster (oben links) sind vermutlich eng miteinander verbunden. Mönche des früheren Benediktinerklosters Ilmmünster sollen möglicherweise schon im 8. Jahrhundert eine klösterliche Außenstelle in Altenstadt gegründet haben. Die lange verbreitete These, dass hier auch das ursprüngliche Dorf Pfaffenhofen entstanden und erst um 1190 einen Kilometer weiter nach Süden verlegt worden ist, wird von Historikern heute allerdings bezweifelt. Aus der Zeit des ehemaligen Ilmmünsterer Klosters ist eine karolingische Chorschranke erhalten geblieben (unten rechts). Eine Kopie davon befindet sich im Pfaffenhofener Heimatmuseum.

The St Andreas church in Altenstadt (top right) and the Romanesque basilica of St Arsatius in Ilmmünster (top left) are probably closely connected. Monks from the former Benedictine monastery in Ilmmünster are believed to have founded a monastic outpost in Altendstadt as long ago as the 8th century. The long propagated theory that this is also where the original village of Pfaffenhofen came into being, and that it was relocated one kilometre further south in 1190, is questioned by historians today. A Carolingian choir screen dating from the time of the former monastery in Ilmmünster has been preserved (bottom right). A copy of it can be seen at the Pfaffenhofen's Museum of Local History.

Das Rentamt am Hauptplatz ist eines der ältesten Gebäude der Stadt. Im Kern stammt es noch aus dem Mittelalter. Nach dem Stadtbrand 1388 hatte Herzog Albrecht III. seine weitgehend zerstörte Hofburg der Stadt Pfaffenhofen zum Bau eines Rathauses überlassen. 1803 verlangte der Staat das Gebäude zurück, um hier das kurfürstliche Rentamt unterzubringen. Später zog das Vermessungsamt in die Räume ein, ehe der Landkreis Pfaffenhofen im Jahr 1976 das historische Gebäude vom Freistaat erwarb.

The revenue office on the main square is one of the oldest buildings in the city. The core of the building dates back to the Middle Ages. After the city fire of 1388, Duke Albrecht III gave what was left of his largely destroyed Imperial Palace to the town of Pfaffenhofen for the building of a town hall. In 1803, the state authorities demanded the return of the building, in order to accommodate the electoral revenue office. The rooms were later occupied by the surveyor's office, before the Pfaffenhofen administrative district acquired the building from the Free State of Bavaria in 1976.

gen, bei ihren Ausgrabungen auch Spuren aus der Zeit unmittelbar vor der ersten urkundlichen Erwähnung des Marktes Pfaffenhofen im 12. Jahrhundert finden zu können, erfüllten sich nicht. „Außer der Jungsteinzeit-Keramik datieren alle anderen bisher ausgewerteten Fundstücke aus der Zeit um 1300 oder später", so Grabungsleiter Bernd Kriens. Deshalb bleiben die näheren Umstände der Ortsgründung nach wie vor ungeklärt.

Über lange Zeit galt die von dem Pfaffenhofener Heimatforscher und Ehrenbürger Heinrich Streidl (1909 – 1989) und anderen Historikern vertretene These als die wahrscheinlichste, dass Pfaffenhofen von Mönchen des im 9. Jahrhundert urkundlich nachgewiesenen Benediktinerklosters Ilmmünster gegründet wurde. Bei Altenstadt, dort wo sich heute der städtische Friedhof und die St. Andreaskirche befinden, sollen die Mönche eine landwirtschaftliche Außenstelle, die Pfaffen-Höfe, errichtet haben. Um 1190 habe dann der Bayernherzog Ludwig der Kelheimer (1173 – 1231) einen Kilometer südlich des ursprünglichen Dorfes Altenstadt, quasi auf der „grünen Wiese", am Zusammenfluss von Ilm und Gerolsbach seinen neuen Markt und Verwaltungssitz gegründet.

So jedenfalls die weit verbreitete Gründungs-Theorie, die allerdings nach Einschätzung von Markus Arnolds nicht mehr haltbar sein dürfte. „Man

Duke Ludwig, and we hope that further excavations will bring new clues to light."

The archaeologist thus supports the theories of Reinhard Haiplik, a local historian, Pfaffenhofen city councillor and secondary-school teacher. Haiplik has, ever since the mid-1990s, taken the view – based on publications by the historians Friedrich Hilble and Volker von Volckamer, as well as on his own detailed studies – that the village of Pfaffenhofen was never moved, but actually originated at its current location. The description used in a document from 1224 for the area around the St Andreas church, *bi der alten stat* ("near the old town"), doesn't refer to a former town called Pfaffenhofen, but merely means *alte Stätte* ("ancient site"). In Haiplik's view, this is probably a reference to a monastic establishment at an ancient place of worship with a sacred spring. However that may be, this was over a long period the site of a well-known therapeutic bath that drew people from all over the country until well into the 16th century. According to Haiplik, there is no written or archaeological evidence that a village settlement also existed next to the spa or the church. He regards the finds from the Neolithic Age unearthed at the Bortenschlager site as another strong indication of the validity of his theory:

Das alte und das vor 200 Jahren eingeführte neue Wappen der Stadt zieren die Ostseite des Turmes der Pfarrkirche St. Johannes Baptist. Im Zuge der Säkularisierung des öffentlichen Lebens hatte die Stadt das ursprüngliche Siegel mit der Darstellung des Pfaffen durch ein neues Hoheitszeichen mit dem Zickzackbalken der Wittelsbacher ersetzt. Auf die später hinzugefügten Verzierungen wie die Krone mit fünf Zinnen, die Pfaffenhofen als Stadt 2. Ranges auswies, wird im amtlichen Stadtwappen heute verzichtet.

The old municipal coat of arms and the new coat of arms introduced 200 years ago grace the east side of the St Johannes Baptist parish church tower. During the secularization of public life, the original seal depicting the cleric was replaced by a new insignia bearing the zigzag line of the Wittelsbach dynasty. The decorative elements added later, such as the crown with five peaks, which designated Pfaffenhofen as a secondary town, no longer form part of today's official coat of arms.

Nahezu noch im Originalzustand erhalten ist dieser 600 Jahre alte Turm an der südlichen Stadtmauer, den der Pfaffenhofener Unternehmer Claus Hipp restaurieren ließ.

For the most part still preserved in its original condition, this 600-year-old tower on the upper city wall was restored by Pfaffenhofen entrepreneur Claus Hipp .

kann wohl davon ausgehen, dass das heutige Stadtgebiet schon lange vor Herzog Ludwig besiedelt war und wir hoffen, bei weiteren Ausgrabungen noch solche Hinweise zu finden. Es spricht jedenfalls wesentlich mehr für die Ortsgründung am heutigen Platz als für die Verlegungstheorie."

Damit stützt der Archäologe die Thesen des Pfaffenhofener Heimatforschers, Stadtrates und Gymnasiallehrers Reinhard Haiplik. Aufgrund von Veröffentlichungen der Historiker Friedrich Hilble und Volker von Volckamer sowie seiner eigenen intensiven Studien vertritt Haiplik schon seit Mitte der 1990er Jahre die Ansicht, dass das Dorf Pfaffenhofen nicht verlegt worden, sondern von Anfang an am heutigen Platz entstanden ist. Die für das Gebiet um die Kirche St. Andreas verwendete Bezeichnung „bi der alten stat" in einer Urkunde aus dem Jahr 1224 weise nicht auf eine ehemalige Stadt Pfaffenhofen hin, sondern bedeute lediglich „alte Stätte". Bei dieser dürfte es sich nach Ansicht Haipliks um die klösterliche Niederlassung an einer uralten Kultstätte mit Quellheiligtum handeln. Jedenfalls gab es an dieser Stelle über lange Zeit ein bekanntes Heilbad, das bis ins 16. Jahrhundert hinein überregionale Zugkraft hatte. Eine „Kurliste" des St. Andreas-Bades aus dem Jahr 1513 dokumentiert 173 Besucher, die zum Teil bis aus Wien, Speyer und Nürnberg anreisten, um hier Heilung und Linderung von ihren Gebrechen und Schmerzen zu erlangen. Irgendwelche schriftliche oder archäologische Nachweise, dass neben dem Heilbad und der Kirche auch eine dörfliche Ansiedlung bestanden hätte, existieren laut Haiplik jedoch nicht. Die Jungsteinzeit-Funde auf dem Bortenschlagerareal wertet er als ein weiteres starkes Indiz für die Richtigkeit seiner Annahme, dass es ein Dorf Pfaffenhofen bei Altenstadt nie gegeben hat, sondern der Ursprung des Ortes immer schon am heutigen Platz lag. „Nach allem, was wir jetzt wissen, ist die Verlegungstheorie jedenfalls sehr, sehr unwahrscheinlich."

Eindeutig geklärt sind die Fragen um die Frühgeschichte der Stadt damit aber nicht. Historisch gesichert ist lediglich, dass Pfaffenhofen in einer Schenkungsurkunde des Klosters Indersdorf aus dem Jahre 1197 erstmals als Markt („foro Pfaffenhovn") erwähnt wird und Herzog Ludwig der Kelheimer in diesem Jahr zu einem Gerichtstag an die Ilm gereist war. Allerdings dürfte Pfaffenhofen schon vor der Regentschaft des 1231 in Kelheim ermordeten Bayernherzogs eine wichtige Funktion für die Grafen von Scheyern, die Ahnherren der Wittelsbacher, erfüllt haben. Fünf Kilometer von deren Stammsitz entfernt, wachten in Pfaffenhofen Dienstmannen, Ritter und Ministerialen von niederem Adel über die Besitzungen der Scheyerer. Um 1159 ist ein Adelbertus de Pfaffenhoven urkundlich erwähnt. Auf ihrer 1224 erstmals bezeugten Wehranlage „Trosperch", die Streidl auf der Anhöhe im Bereich Weihern/Burgfriedenstraße vermutete, hatten die Scheyerer Gefolgsleute wohl für die Sicherheit auf der alten Ilmstraße zu sorgen. Diese war vermutlich schon

that a village called Pfaffenhofen never existed near Altenstadt, and that Pfaffenhofen's current location is also where the original settlement originated. "At any rate, from all that we now know, the relocation theory is highly unlikely."

All that has been preserved historically is that the first mention of Pfaffenhofen, as a market (*foro Pfaffenhovn*), is in a deed of donation dating from 1197 and belonging to the Indersdorf monastery, and that Duke Ludwig the Kelheimer travelled that same year to the Ilm River for a day of judgement. What is likely, however, is that Pfaffenhofen had performed an important function for the counts of Scheyern, the ancestors of the Wittelsbach rulers, even before the regency of the Bavarian duke, who was murdered at Kelheim in 1231. Five kilometres away from the Scheyer ancestral seat, vassals, knights at arms and ministeriales of low nobility stood guard in Pfaffenhofen over the possessions of the Scheyer counts. From their fortifications at "Trosperch" – which Streidl believed was set on the hill near Burgfriedenstrasse in Pfaffenhofen's Weihern district – the Scheyer vassals probably kept law and order along the old Ilm road. This road was presumably a major north-south route even in Roman times, running approximately along the present-day railway line.

When the Scheyer counts moved to Oberwittelsbach near Aichach (around 1106) and their former family seat was converted into a Benedictine monastery (1119), Pfaffenhofen increasingly assumed the function of a local centre of power and administration for the Wittelsbach rulers, who from 1180 on held sway over the Bavarian state without interruption for 700 years as dukes, electors and kings.

As an administrative seat for the Wittelsbachs, Pfaffenhofen fell victim in 1388 to the city war between the allied imperial cities and the Bavarian dukes. As it advanced from Augsburg to Regensburg, the army of the alliance of cities burned the entire market down to the ground, including the ducal palace and parish church. After the locality had been rebuilt and fortified by a 1.5-kilometre-long circular wall, Pfaffenhofen's status was raised from "market" to "town". The first recorded mention of Pfaffenhofen as a town is in a document from 1438. However, the city wall was unable to provide its citizens with lasting protection, for in 1504, during the Landshut War of Succession, palatine mercenaries plundered the town, set fire to houses and killed many of the town's inhabitants.

In 1632, during the Thirty Years' War (1618–48), the plague reached Pfaffenhofen. The pestilence wrought havoc among the population, leaving only 700 survivors out of a population of 1,800. It would take 200 years before the town reached that population level once more. Pfaffenhofen faced difficult times again in April 1745, when Austrian troops,

in der Römerzeit eine wichtige Nord-Süd-Verbindung und verlief ungefähr auf der heutigen Bahntrasse.

Mit dem Umzug der Scheyerer Grafen nach Oberwittelsbach bei Aichach (um 1106) und der Umwandlung ihrer einstigen Stammburg in ein Benediktinerkloster (1119) übernahm Pfaffenhofen mehr und mehr die Funktion eines lokalen Herrschafts- und Verwaltungszentrums für die Wittelsbacher, die ab 1180 ohne Unterbrechung über 700 Jahre als Herzöge, Kurfürsten und Könige das Land Bayern beherrschten.

Als Wittelsbacher-Verwaltungssitz wurde Pfaffenhofen im Jahr 1388 ein Opfer des Städtekrieges zwischen den verbündeten Reichsstädten und den bayerischen Herzögen. Auf dem Vormarsch von Augsburg nach Regensburg brannte das Heer des Städtebundes den gesamten Markt samt herzoglicher Hofburg und Pfarrkirche nieder. Nach dem Wiederaufbau des Ortes und der Befestigung mit einer 1,5 Kilometer langen Ringmauer wurde der Markt Pfaffenhofen zur Stadt erhoben. Die erste Nennung als Stadt findet sich in einer Urkunde aus dem Jahre 1438. Echten Schutz bot die Stadtmauer den Bürgern aber nicht, wie sich schon 1504 während des Landshuter Erbfolgekrieges zeigte, als pfälzische Landsknechte die Stadt plünderten, Häuser in Brand steckten und viele Bewohner töteten.

Während des Dreißigjährigen Krieges (1618-48) kam im Jahr 1632 die Pest nach Pfaffenhofen. Die Seuche wütete schrecklich unter der Bevölkerung. Von den damals 1800 Bewohnern überlebten nur 700. Es dauerte 200 Jahre, bis die Stadt die gleiche Einwohnerzahl wieder erreicht hatte. Schwere Stunden erlebte Pfaffenhofen auch im April 1745, als österreichische Truppen nach der Erstürmung des Münchener Tores die mit dem bayerischen Kurfürsten verbündeten französischen Soldaten aus der Stadt jagten und den Ort plünderten.

Auch Anfang des 19. Jahrhunderts gab es während der napoleonischen Kriege in und um Pfaffenhofen immer wieder Schartmützel zwischen österreichischen und französischen Truppen, zuletzt im April 1809 am Kuglhof, wo ein Marterl heute noch an die gefallenen Soldaten erinnert. Danach blieb die Stadt für lange Zeit von kriegerischen Auseinandersetzungen verschont. Positive Meilensteine in der Entwicklung der Kreisstadt waren vor allem der Bau der Eisenbahnlinie von München nach Ingolstadt in den Jahren 1865 bis 1867 und der Anschluss an die Stromversorgung kurz vor der Jahrhundertwende (ab 1889).

Mit der fortschreitenden Technisierung und dem Aufschwung der heimischen Wirtschaft ging auch ein deutlicher Einwohnerzuwachs einher. Die Bevölkerungszahl, die Mitte des 19. Jahrhunderts gerade erst die 2000er-Grenze überschritten hatte, verdoppelte sich bis zum Jahr 1910 auf 4500. Eine schmerzliche Zäsur brachten die beiden Weltkriege, die in

Der älteste Pfaffenhofener Stadtplan stammt aus dem Jahr 1810. Der Verlauf der wenige Jahre zuvor abgebrochenen Stadtmauer ist noch eindeutig erkennbar, der nach dem Brand von 1388 angelegte mittelalterliche Stadtkern nahezu unverändert erhalten. Nur im Süden (heute Bereich Münchener Vormarkt) hat sich bis zum Jahr 1810 die Bebauung schon stärker ausgedehnt.

The oldest Pfaffenhofen city plan dates from 1810. Still clearly visible is the line followed by the city wall, which had been discontinued just a few years previously, as well as the historic, medieval city centre built after the fire of 1388 and still preserved more or less unchanged. Only in the south (today the Münchener Vormarkt area) had the build-up already developed to a greater degree by 1810.

having stormed the Munich Gate, ran the French soldiers allied with the Bavarian electors out of town and went on a plundering spree.

At the beginning of the 19th century, during the Napoleonic Wars, the Pfaffenhofen area was once again the scene of repeated skirmishes, this time between Austrian and French troops. The last such confrontation occurred in April 1809 at Kuglhof, where a wayside cross still commemorates the fallen soldiers. After that, the town was spared armed conflicts for a long time. Major landmarks in the development of the city as a district capital include the construction of the Munich-to-Ingolstadt railway line between 1865 and 1867, and the city's connection to the electric power supply before the turn of the century (starting in 1889).

Pfaffenhofen um die Wende vom 19. zum 20. Jahrhundert zeigt diese kolorierte Postkarte. Von Nordosten blickt der Maler aus der Vogelperspektive über die 1891 fertig gestellte Bahnstrecke und die damals noch unregulierte Ilm auf die Stadt.
A colourized postcard showing Pfaffenhofen at the turn of the 19th to the 20th century. Viewed from the north-east from a bird's-eye perspective, the artist looks towards the city across the railway line, completed in 1891, and the River Ilm, which was still unregulated at the time.

Ein Luftbild von Hanns Wagner aus dem Jahr 1953 dokumentiert, dass die Stadt allmählich aus dem Zentrum hinauswächst. Auf dem Höhenrücken westlich der Kellerstraße (links unten) sieht man die nach dem Zweiten Weltkrieg errichteten Wohnblöcke der Kreiswohnungsbauhilfe an der Lettner- und Kohnle-Straße.
This aerial photograph taken by Hanns Wagner in 1953 records the city gradually growing outwards from its centre. On the high ridge to the west of Kellerstrasse (bottom left), one can see the blocks of flats that went up after the Second World War on Lettner Strasse and Kohnle Strasse as part of the district housing construction programme.

der Kreisstadt zwar nur relativ geringe materielle Schäden aber viel menschliches Leid in den Familien der Gefallenen, Vermissten und Verwundeten hinterließen.

Der Zustrom der Heimatvertriebenen aus den ehemaligen deutschen Ostgebieten und zahlreicher Neubürger aus anderen Landesteilen sorgte nach dem 2. Weltkrieg zu einem erheblichen Einwohnerzuwachs in Pfaffenhofen. Lebten hier bei der Volkszählung 1939 noch 5292 Bürger, so stieg deren Zahl nach Kriegsende auf rund 7000 an.

Die Zehntausender-Marke übersprang Pfaffenhofen aber erst mit der Gemeindegebietsreform in den Jahren 1971 bis 1978. Nach der Eingliederung der einstmals zwölf selbstständigen Gemeinden Eberstetten, Affalterbach, Angkofen, Ehrenberg, Förnbach, Gundamsried, Haimpertshofen, Sulzbach, Tegernbach, Uttenhofen, Walkersbach und zuletzt Niederscheyern lebten am 1. Mai 1978 auf einer vergrößerten Fläche von 93 Quadratkilometern nun rund 15 000 Einwohner.

Aber nicht nur die politisch mehr oder weniger erzwungenen Eingemeindungen ließen Pfaffenhofen in immer schnellerem Tempo wachsen, sondern auch der stärkere Zuzug von Neubürgern. Besonders deutlich zeigte sich dieser Trend Ende der 1980er und Anfang der 1990er Jahre, als die Einwohnerzahl (auch wegen vieler Zuwanderer aus den neuen Bundesländern) um durchschnittlich 500 jährlich auf 21 300 anstieg.

Ab der zweiten Hälfte der 1990er Jahre vollzog sich das Wachstum der Stadt wieder in ruhigeren Bahnen mit durchschnittlich knapp 200 Einwohnern pro Jahr. Zu Beginn des Jahres 2012 lebten in Pfaffenhofen 24 124 Menschen, davon drei Viertel in der Kernstadt und rund 6000 in den Ortsteilen.

The upswing in the local economy was accompanied by a marked population increase: having topped 2,000 by the mid-19th century, the population more than doubled to 4,500 by 1910. But the two world wars proved a painful turning point for the city, causing relatively little material damage but a great deal of human suffering for the families of those who died, went missing or were wounded in the conflict.

The influx of expellees from Germany's former eastern territories after the Second World War prompted a noticeable increase in Pfaffenhofen's population. Whereas the 1939 census listed 5,292 citizens, by war's end this figure had risen to around 7,000, but it would take until the municipal territory reform of 1971 to 1978 before Pfaffenhofen passed the 10,000 mark. After the incorporation of the 12 formerly independent municipalities of Eberstetten, Affalterbach, Angkofen, Ehrenberg, Förnbach, Gundamsried, Haimpertshofen, Sulzbach, Tegernbach, Uttenhofen, Walkersbach and Niederscheyern, by 1 May 1978 there were a total of about 15,000 inhabitants living on an enlarged area of 93 square kiliometres. But the incorporations weren't the only reason for Pfaffenhofen's high-speed growth; the greater inflow of new inhabitants also contributed to the increases. This trend was especially evident at the beginning of the 1990s, when the total population increased annually by an average of 500 (also because of the many immigrants from Germany's new eastern states) to reach a new high of 21,300.

From the second half of the 1990s on, the city continued to grow at a more leisurely pace once again, averaging almost 200 new residents a year. At the beginning of 2012, Pfaffenhofen had 24,124 inhabitants – three quarters of them living in the city proper, and about 6,000 in its villages.

Pfaffenhofen im Mai 2012. Die Bebauung hat sich vor allem nach Westen enorm ausgedehnt. Sogar westlich der Trabrennbahn und der 1973/74 gebauten Umgehungsstraße sind im Ortsteil Sulzbach neue große Siedlungsgebiete entstanden.

Pfaffenhofen in May 2012. The city's expansion is especially large towards the west. New and large settlement areas have even been developed in the Sulzbach part of the city, west of the trotting race course and the bypass built in 1973/74.

4 SCHÖNER LEBEN AN DER ILM
A MORE BEAUTIFUL LIFE ON THE RIVER ILM

Was den LivCom-Award-Sieger Pfaffenhofen so lebens- und liebenswert macht

31. Oktober 2011, kurz nach 15 Uhr: Solche Jubelszenen hat der ehrwürdige Festsaal des Pfaffenhofener Rathauses in seiner fast 150-jährigen Geschichte wohl selten erlebt. 2. Bürgermeister Albert Gürtner, Wirtschaftsreferent Markus Käser und Kulturreferent Steffen Kopetzky springen von ihren Stühlen auf, reißen die Arme jubelnd in die Höhe. Fahnen in den Stadtfarben blau-gelb werden geschwenkt. Auch viele Mitarbeiter der Stadtverwaltung und Pfaffenhofener Bürger, die sich vor der Videoleinwand im Rathaussaal versammelt haben, klatschen in die Hände und hüpfen vor Begeisterung über das Eichenparkett, als der Jury-Präsident per Internet-Live-Stream aus der südkoreanischen Hauptstadt Seoul das Ergebnis verkündet: Pfaffenhofen an der Ilm ist Sieger des internationalen LivCom-Awards und darf sich künftig mit dem Titel „lebenswerteste Stadt der Welt 2011" in der Kategorie von 20 000 bis 75 000 Einwohner schmücken. Und dazu auch noch mit einem Sonderpreis für vorbildliches Umweltmanagement.

Pfaffenhofen? Durchreisende registrieren den Namen nur flüchtig im Vorbeifahren auf den Schildern an der Autobahn bei Schweitenkirchen. Oder sie hören ihn in den Verkehrsfunk-Durchsagen im Radio. Aber sonst nehmen Fremde kaum Notiz von dem Ort, der da irgendwo hinter den Hügeln und Hopfenstangen abseits der Fernstraße A9 liegt. Gerne verwechseln Ortsunkundige die Hallertauer Kreisstadt auch mit Oberpfaffenhofen im Landkreis Starnberg. Es ist zwar zehnmal kleiner als Pfaffenhofen an der Ilm, hat als Standort des Deutschen Forschungszentrums für Luft- und Raumfahrt (DLR) aber schon seit Jahrzehnten eine starke überregionale Medienpräsenz. Bei 20 weiteren Orten namens Pfaffenhofen allein im süddeutsch-österreichischen Raum ist ihre richtige geographische Einordnung auch nicht ganz einfach.

Seit Pfaffenhofen an der Ilm aber als einziger deutscher Vertreter am Finale des von den Vereinten Nationen geförderten LivCom-Awards 2011 in Seoul teilnehmen und dort zwei Trophäen gewinnen konnte, ist der Bekanntheitsgrad der Kreisstadt immens gestiegen. Es gab kaum eine Zeitung, TV- oder Radioanstalt von Flensburg bis Mittenwald, die im Herbst 2011 nicht über die lebenswerteste Stadt der Welt berichtete.

LivCom Award winner – what makes Pfaffenhofen so liveable and loveable

31 October 2011, shortly after 3 p.m. It's unlikely that the dignified banqueting hall at Pfaffenhofen's town hall has ever witnessed such scenes of celebration in all of its 150-year history. Albert Gürtner, the deputy mayor, Markus Käser, the councillors in charge, and Steffen Kopetzky, of the city's economic department and the arts, have leapt out of their chairs and are thrusting their arms into the air out of sheer jubilation. People are waving flags of blue and yellow, the city's colours, and the many municipal administration employees and local citizens who have gathered in front of a video screen in the council chamber are clapping their hands and hopping excitedly across the oak parquet. The cause of all this excitement is the live stream announcement by the jury president in the South Korean capital (Seoul) that Pfaffenhofen an der Ilm has won an International LivCom Award, making it the proud bearer of the title "Most Liveable City in the World 2011" in the category 20,000 to 75,000 inhabitants, and has also been awarded a special prize for "Environmental Best Practice".

Pfaffenhofen, you ask? Travellers only briefly register the name of the city on road signs along the A9 motorway near Schweitenkirchen, or perhaps hear the name mentioned in radio broadcasts of traffic information. Otherwise, they barely notice the place, which lies somewhere off the A9 behind those hills and hop poles. Non-locals readily mistake this major district town in the Hallertau region for Oberpfaffenhofen, in the Starnberg district. Although Oberpfaffenhofen is only a tenth the size of Pfaffenhofen an der Ilm, it has for decades enjoyed a strong media presence throughout the country thanks to its being the location of the German Aerospace Centre. Given that there are 20 other Pfaffenhofens in Southern Germany and Austria alone, it's no wonder that people find it difficult to pinpoint this particular city geographically.

However, as the only German representative in the finals of the UN-sponsored LivCom Awards in Seoul and a winner of two of its trophies, Pfaffenhofen's profile as a district capital has increased immensely. From Flensburg in the north to Mittenwald in the south of the country, there was hardly a newspaper, TV or radio station that did not report on the world's most liveable city in the autumn of 2011. It's thanks to this huge media

Wir lieben Pfaffenhofen! Luftballons in den Stadtfarben gelb-blau schicken große und kleine Fans der Kreisstadt für die offizielle Videopräsentation zum LivCom-Award in den Himmel.
We love Pfaffenhofen! Large and small fans of this district capital releasing yellow and blue balloons (the city's colours) into the air in October 2011 to mark the official video presentation for the LivCom Awards.

Und dank des riesigen Medienechos wissen nun wesentlich mehr Menschen im Rest der Republik, dass das Städtchen Pfaffenhofen in der schönen Hallertau liegt und ein Fluss mit dem Namen Ilm nicht nur durch die Goethestadt Weimar, sondern auch durch das nördliche Oberbayern fließt.

Der Erfolg der bisher wenig bekannten Kreisstadt im Herzen Bayerns überraschte nicht nur Beobachter außerhalb des Landkreises. Auch so mancher alt eingesessene Pfaffenhofener fragte sich verwundert, weshalb eine internationale Experten-Jury ausgerechnet seine Heimatgemeinde als lebenswerteste Stadt gekürt - und darüber hinaus auch noch gegen prominente Konkurrenz wie Bordeaux, Bilbao, die Provinz Siena oder die chinesische Millionenstadt Nanjing mit einem Sonderpreis für vorbildliches Umweltmanagement dekoriert hatte. Schließlich ist der typische Pfaffenhofener im Alltag eher geneigt, sich über Hundehäufchen oder Schlaglöcher aufzuregen, als mit Stolz geschwellter Brust auf seine Stadt zu schauen – getreu dem in Bayern weit verbreiteten Motto „ned g'schimpft is g'lobt gnua".

Dass mit dem Gewinn des LivCom-Awards viele Pfaffenhofener ihre Heimatstadt plötzlich in einem wesentlich positiveren Licht sahen, ist neben dem überregionalen Imagegewinn wohl der erfreulichste Effekt der Auszeichnung in Seoul. Machte der Titelgewinn doch vielen Bewohnern erst richtig bewusst, wie lebens- und liebenswert ihre Heimatstadt ist und welch hohe Lebensqualität sie hier vorfinden.

Wie sich ihr persönliches Pfaffenhofen-Bild verändert hat, beschreibt die an der Ilm aufgewachsene und heute in Hongkong lebende Journalistin Lisa von Ortenberg in der Wochenzeitung „Welt am Sonntag" vom 6. November 2011: „Ich gestehe, dass ich mit 20 auch fast alle Städte reizvoller fand, als PAF. Ich war auch überrascht, als ich hörte, dass Pfaffenhofen jetzt von den Vereinten Nationen zur lebenswertesten Kleinstadt der Welt erklärt worden ist. Aber im Grunde ist mir, seit ich weg bin und mit wachsender räumlicher Distanz, immer klarer geworden, welch liebenswerte Stadt meine Heimatstadt doch ist".

Auch bei der öffentlichen Siegesfeier, zu der eine Woche nach dem LivCom-Finale Tausende von Bürgern vor das Rathaus strömten, war ganz deutlich zu spüren: Die Pfaffenhofener sind stolz auf ihre Heimatstadt und haben ein neues Wir-Gefühl entdeckt. Darüber freut sich besonders der Pfaffenhofener Bürgermeister Thomas Herker, der als 29-jähriger SPD-Newcomer im Jahr 2008 mit einer bunten Koalition aus Sozialdemokraten, Freien Wählern, Grünen und ödp die Führung im zuvor „schwarz" regierten Rathaus übernahm. Er weiß genau, dass die Pfaffenhofener Erfolgsstory vor allem einem glücklichen Umstand zu verdanken ist: der bevorzugten geografischen Lage im Herzen des Freistaates

response that considerably more people throughout Germany now know that this town lies in the beautiful Hallertau region – and that in addition to the River Ilm that flows through Goethe's Weimar, there's another river of the same name flowing through the northern part of Upper Bavaria..

It was not only observers outside the region who were surprised by the success of this little-known district capital in the heart of Bavaria. Many a veteran Pfaffenhofen resident must have wondered why an international jury of experts would choose their local community of all places as the most liveable city – and, as if that weren't enough, also award it a special prize for exemplary environmental management in the face of competition from prominent rivals such as Bordeaux, Bilbao, the province of Siena and the megacity Nanjing. After all, in everyday life, the typical Pfaffenhofen inhabitant is more inclined to get worked up over dog doos or potholes in the road than to puff out his chest with pride at the sight of his city – along the lines of "Not being scolded is praise enough", as Bavarians like to say.

The fact that many Pfaffenhofen citizens were suddenly able to see their home town in a much more positive light was – besides the nationwide image boost – probably the most gratifying aspect of winning the LivCom Award in Seoul. For it did indeed make many of Pfaffenhofen's residents really aware for the first time just how liveable and loveable their home town is, and what a high quality of life it affords them.

In the *Welt am Sonntag* weekly of 6 November 2011, the journalist Lisa von Ortenberg, who grew up in the Ilm area but now lives in Hong Kong, describes how her personal view of Pfaffenhofen has changed: "I admit that at the age of 20 I found almost all other towns more appealing than 'PAF.' I was as surprised as anyone else to hear that the United Nations had named Pfaffenhofen the world's most liveable small city. But deep down, ever since I left and as the distance has grown greater, it's become increasingly clear how loveable my home town is after all."

For the thousands of locals who flocked to the Town Hall a week after the LivCom final, there was still a clearly palpable feeling that Pfaffenhofen citizens are proud of their home town and have discovered a new "we" feeling of belonging. One person who's particularly delighted about this is the mayor of Pfaffenhofen, Thomas Herker, who was a 29-year-old SPD newcomer when he took office in 2008 at the head of a colourful coalition of Social Democrats, Free Voters, Greens, and the Ecological Democratic Party, replacing Bavaria's Christian Social Union. He's fully aware that Pfaffenhofen's success story is due primarily to a fortunate circumstance: its privileged geographical location at the heart of the Free State of Bavaria, right at the centre of the Munich metropolitan region, one of Europe's most attractive and most successful economic areas. A

Bürgermeister Thomas Herker nimmt in der südkoreanischen Hauptstadt Seoul die Siegertrophäe des LivCom-Awards in der Kategorie bis 75 000 Einwohner entgegen (oben rechts).

Foto oben links: Kulturreferent Steffen Kopetzky, Wirtschaftsreferent Markus Käser und 2. Bürgermeister Albert Gürtner (von rechts) bejubeln mit vielen Bürgern im Rathaussaal die Bekanntgabe des LivCom-Erfolges.

Triumphale Heimkehr: Nach der Landung auf dem Flughafen München bereiten die Pfaffenhofener ihrem Bürgermeister Thomas Herker und Matthias Scholz, Geschäftsführer der Wirtschafts- und Servicegesellschaft, einen herzlichen Empfang (Bild unten).

Mayor Thomas Herker accepting the winners' trophy at the LivCom Awards in the South Korean capital, Seoul, for the category "up to 75,000 inhabitants" (top right).

Photo top left: Steffen Kopetzky, the city councillor in charge of the arts, Markus Käser, city councillor of the economic department, and Deputy Mayor Albert Gürtner (from right to left) cheering the LivCom announcement with many local residents gathered in the council chamber at the town hall.

Triumphal homecoming: after landing at Munich airport, Mayor Thomas Herker and Matthias Scholz, Managing Director of the Wirtschaftsservice Gesellschaft, are given a warm welcome by Pfaffenhofen citizens (bottom picture).

Neue Siedlungen, wie hier im Baugebiet Radlhöfe, schaffen Wohnraum für die zahlreichen Neubürger.
New housing estates, like the one here in the Radlhöfe building area, provide living space for many new inhabitants.

Bayern, mittendrin in der Metropolregion München, einem der zugkräftigsten und erfolgreichsten Wirtschaftsräume Europas. Ein gesunder Branchenmix mit Industriebetrieben, mittelständischen Unternehmen, Handel, Handwerk und Dienstleistern verhilft Pfaffenhofen wie auch den meisten anderen Städten und Gemeinden im Landkreis seit Jahren zu kräftig sprudelnden Steuereinnahmen. Wie gut die Ilmstadt wirtschaftlich dasteht, verdeutlichen Zahlen aus dem Haushalt 2012: Die finanziellen Rücklagen der Stadt waren zum Jahresbeginn mit 14,2 Millionen Euro deutlich höher als die Verschuldung in Höhe von 11,2 Millionen Euro. Auch ohne Berücksichtigung der vorhandenen Geldreserven lag die Pfaffenhofener Pro-Kopf-Verschuldung mit 460 Euro noch weit unter dem Landesdurchschnitt (1006 Euro im Jahr 2010). Die grundsoliden Kommunal-Finanzen und die florierende mittelständische Wirtschaft bringen der Region auch regelmäßig Spitzenplätze in Arbeitsmarkt-Statistiken und Vergleichsstudien zur wirtschaftlichen Leistungskraft ein. So belegte Pfaffenhofen im Dezember 2011 beim Ranking des Wirtschaftsmagazins Focus Money den ersten Platz unter rund 400 Landkreisen und kreisfreien Städten in ganz Deutschland.

Die Arbeitslosenqoute des Landkreises Pfaffenhofen lag im April

healthy mix of industrial plants, medium-sized businesses, commerce, crafts and service providers has for years ensured an equally healthy flow of tax revenues for Pfaffenhofen and most of the other towns and communities in the district. A few figures from Pfaffenhofen's 2012 budget serve to illustrate how well off the city on the Ilm is economically: at the beginning of the year, its financial reserves of 14.2 million euros were significantly higher than its total debts of 11.2 million euros. Even without taking into account existing cash reserves, Pfaffenhofen's 2010 per capita indebtedness of 460 euros per resident is well below the state average for Bavaria (1,006 euros in 2010). Such rock-solid community finances and the flourishing medium-sized business sector also regularly earn the region top placings in labour-market statistics and comparative studies on economic strength. In December 2011, for example, Pfaffenhofen came top of a list of 400 administrative and urban districts surveyed throughout Germany by the business magazine *Focus Money*.

In April 2012, the unemployment rate in the Pfaffenhofen district was 2.0 per cent, second only to Eichstätt (1.2 per cent) – a superlative ranking in the Free State of Bavaria, where the average rate of unemployment was 3.7 per cent (7.0 per cent at the national level).

Its central location 50 km north of Munich, 30 km south of Ingolstadt and about 70 km from Augsburg and Regensburg, its close proximity to Munich Airport 2 and excellent transport connections to the A9 and A93 motorways, as well as the Munich-to-Nuremberg railway line all go to make Pfaffenhofen an attractive proposition for companies – a "fertile ground for major investments" was the city's bold claim when it filed its application for the LivCom Award. Notable examples are the baby food manufacturer Hipp and the Japanese pharmaceutical company Daiichi Sankyo, who together employ around 1,500 people.

An important future objective for local politicians and the WSP business funding company will be to market the city's locational advantage even more successfully and locate other companies offering highly skilled jobs to Pfaffenhofen. After all, in 2012, some 5,000 Pfaffenhofen residents were still commuting out of the district every day to their place of work, mainly in Munich and Ingolstadt.

2012 bei 2,0 Prozent, hinter dem Spitzenreiter Eichstätt (1,2 Prozent) ein Topwert im Freistaat Bayern, wo sich die durchschnittliche Arbeitslosenquote auf 3,7 Prozent belief (im Bund 7,0 %).

Die zentrale Lage 50 Kilometer nördlich von München, 30 Kilometer südlich von Ingolstadt und jeweils etwa 70 Kilometer von Augsburg und Regensburg entfernt, aber auch die Nähe zum Flughafen München 2 und die optimale Verkehrsanbindung mit den Autobahnen A9 und A93 sowie die Bahnlinie München-Nürnberg, machen Pfaffenhofen zu einem attraktiven Standort für Unternehmen. Sie finden hier einen „guten Boden für große Vorhaben“, wie es die Stadt in ihrer Bewerbung zum LivCom-Award plakativ formuliert hatte. Beispiele dafür sind vor allem der Babynahrungshersteller Hipp und der japanische Pharmakonzern Daiichi Sankyo, die in Pfaffenhofen insgesamt rund 1500 Menschen beschäftigen.

Den Standortvorteil noch besser zu vermarkten und weitere Firmen mit qualifizierten Arbeitsplätzen in Pfaffenhofen anzusiedeln, wird auch in Zukunft ein wichtiges Anliegen der Kommunalpolitik und der städtischen Wirtschafts- und Servicegesellschaft (WSP) sein. Denn rund 5000 Pfaffenhofener pendelten im Jahr 2012 noch täglich an ihre Arbeitsplätze außerhalb des Landkreises, vorwiegend nach München und Ingolstadt.

Wie lebenswert eine Kommune in ländlichen Regionen ist, bemisst sich für die Bewohner vor allem daran, dass sie hier nicht nur günstigen Wohnraum finden, sondern auch Arbeitsplätze, attraktive Einkaufsmöglichkeiten, Kultur-, Sport- und Freizeiteinrichtungen, Schulen, eine hochwertige medizinische Versorgung und alle sonst noch wichtigen Einrichtungen des täglichen Bedarfs.

Mit dem Zug oder – wenn es gut läuft – auch mit dem Auto in einer halben Stunde die Großstädte zu erreichen, birgt für die Kommunen im Umland die Gefahr, die eigene Identität zu verlieren und immer mehr zur Schlafstadt zu verkommen. Dies haben viele Gemeinden gerade im Einzugsbereich der Münchener S-Bahn schon schmerzvoll erfahren müssen. Wie sollen zum Beispiel die Fachgeschäfte in Kleinstädten noch überleben, wenn die Kunden zunehmend in die Fußgängerzonen und Einkaufszentren der nahe gelegenen Großstädte abwandern? Die Klage über den wachsenden Kaufkraft-Abfluss und eine Verödung von Handel und Gewerbe im Stadtzentrum war über Jahre hinweg ein beherrschendes kommunalpolitisches Thema auch in Pfaffenhofen. Ebenso wie das mühsame Streben der örtlichen Kultur-Szene, im Schatten des übermächtigen Münchener und Ingolstädter Musik-, Theater- und Kunstbetriebes auch über die Pfaffenhofener Stadtgrenzen hinaus noch wahrgenommen zu werden.

Mitten im Herzen Bayerns liegt Pfaffenhofen zwischen den Ballungsräume München, Ingolstadt und Augsburg.

Pfaffenhofen lies in the heart of Bavaria between the Munich, Ingolstadt and Augsburg conurbations.

Die nahe gelegenen Autobahnen A9 und A93 mit der Anschlussstelle bei Schweitenkirchen und dem Holledauer Dreieck sind ein wesentlicher Standortvorteil für Pfaffenhofen.
The nearby A9 and A93 motorways with the junction for Schweitenkirchen and the Holledau triangle are an important locational advantage for Pfaffenhofen.

How liveable local communities in rural regions are for their inhabitants is measured primarily by access they have not only to affordable housing, but also to jobs, attractive shopping opportunities, cultural, sporting and recreational facilities, schools, high-quality health care services, as well as all the other important facilities required to meet daily needs.

When the nearest large cities can be reached within half an hour by train or even by car, local communities in the surrounding area run the risk of losing their own identity and being reduced more and more to the status of a dormitory suburb. This has already been the painful experience of many municipalities located along the commuter belt of

Im Gegensatz zu manch anderen Orten im Einzugsgebiet der Ballungszentren hat man in Pfaffenhofen aber den schwierigen Spagat geschafft, von den Vorteilen der Großstadtnähe zu profitieren und dabei nicht die Identität als eigenständige, lebendige Kleinstadt zu verlieren. In den Wochen vor dem LivCom-Finale im Herbst 2011 hatte die örtliche Lokalzeitung „Pfaffenhofener Kurier" ihre Leserinnen und Leser in Kurzinterviews befragt, warum die Stadt für sie so lebenswert ist. Der 71-jährige Lothar Lehmann, vor 40 Jahren mit seiner Frau Rosemarie aus der Landeshauptstadt an die Ilm gezogen, erklärte, was ihm an Pfaffenhofen besonders gefällt: „Weil es sich von einem verschlafenen Dorf zu einer pulsierenden Stadt entwickelt hat...Und das Schönste an München ist die Autobahn nach Pfaffenhofen". Die augenzwinkernde Schlussbemerkung verdeutlicht, wie wohl sich die Bewohner heute in ihrer Stadt fühlen.

Dass Heimatliebe und Lokalpatriotismus durchaus berechtigt sind, hat die Stadt mit der Verleihung des LivCom-Awards nun auch von neutralen internationalen Experten bestätigt bekommen. Anhand von sechs Aufgabenfeldern hatte die Jury in Seoul durchleuchtet, wie umweltbewusst, bürgerfreundlich und zukunftsfähig die Kommune bereits ist und durch welche Maßnahmen sie künftig noch lebenswerter werden will. Die Förderung von Kunst und Kultur sowie die Bewahrung des historischen Erbes gehörten ebenso zu dem Kriterienkatalog wie die lokalen Maßnahmen zum Natur- und Klimaschutz, die Beteiligung der Bürger an kommunalen Entscheidungen, das Angebot im medizinischen und sozialen Bereich sowie das ehrenamtliche Engagement.

Das für die meisten Bürger wohl augenfälligste Beispiel, wo sich die Pfaffenhofener Lebensqualität in den letzten Jahren am deutlichsten verbessert hat, ist der Hauptplatz, seit Jahrhunderten das Zentrum der Hallertauer Kreisstadt. Mit der zunehmenden Motorisierung, vor allem ab den 1970er Jahren, war der schöne Platz zu einer Blechwüste verkommen. Fußgänger und Radfahrer, insbesondere Mütter mit kleineren Kindern, erlebten es als tägliches Ärgernis, sich zwischen fahrenden und parkenden Autos durchschlängeln zu müssen. Jahrzehntelang diskutierten Bürger und Kommunalpolitiker kontrovers über eine Verkehrsberuhigung und Umgestaltung des Platzes. Die Befürworter einer Fußgängerzone stritten erbittert mit den Einzelhändlern, die sich vehement gegen eine Reduzierung der Parkplätze und für freie Fahrt der Autos durch das Zentrum einsetzten. Der Streit um den Bau einer Tiefgarage unter dem Hauptplatz, die im Jahr 1998 mit hauchdünner Mehrheit in einem Bürgerentscheid befürwortet worden war, letztendlich aber an technischen und finanziellen Problemen scheiterte, lähmte über viele Jahre hinweg die Kommunalpolitik. Bis der Stadtrat nach zahlreichen mehr oder weniger gelungenen Kompromisslösungen und kosmetischen Verbesserungen im

Munich's suburban railway system. How, for example, are specialist shops in small towns expected to survive if their customers continue to migrate to the pedestrian precincts and shopping centres of nearby big cities? For several years now, complaints about the increasing draining away of purchasing power and the effect of deserted town centres on local trade and commerce have also been a dominant topic in local politics in Pfaffenhofen. The same goes for the arduous efforts by the local cultural scene to establish a profile beyond Pfaffenhofen itself, living as it does in the shadows of the mightier music, theatre and art worlds of Munich and Ingolstadt.

Unlike many other places along the commuter belt of conurbation hubs, Pfaffenhofen has managed to master a difficult balancing act between benefiting from the advantages of its proximity to a large city without at the same time losing its own identity as a lively, independent small city. In the weeks prior to the LivCom final in 2011, the local newspaper *Pfaffenhofener Kurier* had conducted brief interviews with its readers, asking them what made their city so liveable. One of those interviewed, 71-year-old Lothar Lehmann, had moved to Pfaffenhofen from Munich with his wife, Rosemarie, four decades previously. What he found so special about his adopted home town was that it had "developed from a sleepy village into a pulsating city ... and that the best thing about Munich was the motorway to Pfaffenhofen". The tongue-in-cheek closing remark illustrates how well the locals feel in their city.

With the presentation of the LivCom Award, Pfaffenhofen now also had confirmation from a neutral panel of international experts that love of one's homeland and local patriotism is thoroughly justified. Based on six fields of activity, the Seoul jury took a close look at how environmentally conscious, citizen-friendly and sustainable the local community already is, and what Pfaffenhofen was planning to do to make it even more liveable. The support and promotion of the arts and culture and the preservation of the city's historical heritage were just as much part of the jury's list of criteria as were the local measures to protect the climate and environment, the active participation of citizens in local decision-making, the range of services available in the medical and social sectors, and the level of voluntary community involvement.

For most Pfaffenhofen citizens, probably the most obvious example of where their quality of life has improved most noticeably in recent years is the main square, for centuries the centre of life in the Hallertau region's district capital. Increasing motorization, especially from the 1970s onwards, had turned this beautiful square into a sea of metal – a daily nuisance for pedestrians and cyclists, and for mothers with small children in particular, who were forced to weave their way between

e Neugestaltung des Pfaffenhofener Hauptplatzes war in den Jahren 2008/2009 die itialzündung für die Belebung der Pfaffenhofener Innenstadt. Der 300 Meter lange Platz ist mit ner Fläche von 1,5 Hektar ungefähr doppelt so groß wie die Münchener Allianzarena.

The redesign of Pfaffenhofen's main square in 2008/09 had a vitalizing effect on the city centre as a whole. 300 metres long and with an area of 1,5 hectares, the square is roughly twice the size of the Allianz Arena football stadium in Munich.

Eingerahmt von den historischen Fassaden des alten Rentamtes (links) und der Bäckerei Bergmeister setzt der Geschäfts- und Verwaltungsneubau am Sigleck einen modernen Akzent.
Framed by the historic facades of the old revenue office (left) and the Bergmeister bakery, a modern architectural accent is added by the new commercial and administration building at the Sigleck.

Lebensraum Hauptplatz: Seit der Neugestaltung gibt es nun mehr Raum zum Verweilen und Flanieren.
Life on the main square: since its redesign, there's a lot more space in which to linger and stroll around.

April 2007 unter dem damaligen CSU-Bürgermeister Hans Prechter endlich den Mut hatte, Nägel mit Köpfen zu machen und den Beschluss zur grundlegenden Umgestaltung fasste.

In den Jahren 2008 und 2009 wurde die Platzarchitektur nach Plänen des Ingenieurbüros Klaus Immich mit Granitpflaster, einer kleineren Grünanlage, zwei Brunnen und großzügigeren Fußgängerbereichen neu konzipiert. Erheblich weniger Parkplätze und ein striktes Durchfahrtsverbot für Kraftfahrzeuge am Rathaus waren die Grundlagen für die Umsetzung des Konzepts, das heute sogar von den einstigen Kritikern und Skeptikern als Erfolg gesehen wird. Wo früher, vor allem während der Wochenmärkte am Dienstag und Samstag, die Autos noch Stoßstange an Stoßstange über den Asphalt rollten, planschen heute Kinder in den Wasserfontänen eines Flachbrunnens, den die Stadt in der Fußgängerzone vor dem Rathaus angelegt hat. In den Straßencafes und an den Wirtshaustischen, die sich auf dem Platz immer weiter ausbreiten, genießen derweil die Pfaffenhofener ihren Cappuccino, ein Weißbier oder frische Weißwürste und Brezen vom Metzger und Bäcker gleich nebenan.

Mit wesentlich weniger störendem Blech, Lärm und Benzingestank hat der Hauptplatz seinen ursprünglichen städtebaulichen Charakter und Charme wieder zurück gewonnen. An schönen Sommertagen, insbesondere wenn auf dem Wochenmarkt die Bauern aus der Umgebung neben den Obst-, Gemüse- und Feinkosthändlern ihre Produkte feilbieten und der Duft von gegrillten Bratwürsten, Schaschlik und Hähnchen über den Platz zieht, gleicht die Szenerie dem bunten Treiben auf einer italienischen Piazza.

Vom neugotischen Rathaus auf der Ostseite erstreckt sich der Platz fast 300 Meter nach Westen bis zur Stadtpfarrkirche St. Johannes mit ihrem hoch aufragenden gotischen Turm und dem Haus der Begegnung. Die imposante Platzarchitektur stammt noch aus dem Mittelalter und zeugt von der schon damals beachtlichen Bedeutung der Stadt als wichtiger Verwaltungssitz der Wittelsbacher Fürsten sowie vom Wohlstand und Selbstbewusstsein ihrer Bewohner. Seit der Umgestaltung des Platzes kommt die beeindruckende Kulisse wesentlich besser zur Geltung als zuvor mit den großkronigen Kastanienbäumen und kreuz und quer parkenden Autos, die das Straßenbild beherrschten. Wohl zu recht gilt der Pfaffenhofener Hauptplatz heute mehr denn je als einer der schönsten Stadtplätze Oberbayerns.

Die Neugestaltung des Platzes wirkte auch als Initialzündung für weitere zukunftsweisende Investitionen im Stadtzentrum wie dem Neubau eines Geschäfts- und Verwaltungsgebäudes auf dem lange Zeit ungenutzten Franzbräu- und Siglareal an der Ingolstädter Straße. Mit

In ständig wechselnden Farben wird in den Abendstunden das Wasserspiel in der Fußgängerzone vor dem Rathaus effektvoll beleuchtet.
In the pedestrian precinct, the water fountain in front of the town hall is strikingly illuminated at night with constantly changing colours.

moving vehicles and parked cars. For decades, traffic reduction and a redesign of the square became the subject of controversial public discussion between the townspeople and local politicians. Those in favour of a pedestrian zone became embroiled in acrimonious disputes with retail traders, who vehemently resisted any reduction in the number of parking spaces and advocated allowing cars to move freely through the city centre. The dispute over plans to construct an underground car park beneath the main square – approved by a wafer-thin majority in a 1998 referendum but eventually dropped because of technical and financial problems – paralysed local politics for many years. Until April 2007 that is, when the city council, led by the then mayor, Hans Prechter, finally found the courage to "get its act together" and, after numerous more or less successful compromise solutions and cosmetic improvements, passed a resolution to fundamentally transform the square.

In 2008 and 2009, the architecture of the public square was completely redesigned according to plans by the engineering office of Klaus Immich providing for granite paving setts, a somewhat smaller green park, two fountains, and more spacious pedestrian areas. The underlying concept behind the plans foresaw a significant reduction in the number of parking spaces and a strict ban on motor vehicles near the town hall, a concept that even former critics and opponents now regard as a success. Where cars once rolled bumper to bumper across the asphalt, especially on market day every Tuesday and Saturday, children now splash around in the water fountains of a shallow well, installed by the city in the pedestrian zone in front of the town hall. In the meantime, Pfaffenhofen locals are able to enjoy a cappuccino or weissbier, or fresh weisswurst and pretzels supplied by the butcher and baker next door, at any of the increasing number of street cafés and pubs in the square.

Without all that metal and noise and the constant reek of petrol, the main square has regained its original character and charm. On any beautiful summer's day, especially when farmers from the surrounding areas are in town to sell their products alongside the fruit and vegetable sellers and delicatessen food suppliers, and the scent of grilled bratwurst, shashlik and chicken wafts across the square, the scene resembles the colourful hustle and bustle of an Italian piazza.

dem Beschluss, die Büroflächen in den Obergeschossen des Neubaus für die Stadtverwaltung zu erwerben, machte der Stadtrat den Weg für den Investor Hans Baierl (Trend Immobilien) frei, sein lange aufgeschobenes Projekt zu realisieren. Um die dafür erforderlichen zusätzlichen Parkplätze zu schaffen, packte Baierl in den Jahren 2010 und 2011 eine weitere große Baumaßnahme im Stadtzentrum an: Auf dem Gelände des ehemaligen Hotels Bortenschlager, das ebenfalls jahrelang brach gelegen war, entstanden zwischen Hauptplatz und Auenstraße attraktive Verkaufsflächen, Büroräume für Arbeitsagentur und Jobcenter sowie ein modernes Parkhaus mit 160 Stellplätzen.

So sehr sich die Pfaffenhofener auch über die neuen Einkaufsmagneten und die Belebung der Innenstadt freuen, bedauern doch viele, dass mit Siglbräu und Hotel Bortenschlager wieder zwei traditionsreiche und mit zahlreichen persönlichen Erinnerungen verbundene Urgesteine der lokalen Wirtshauskultur für immer aus dem Stadtbild verschwunden sind. Aber wie hätte man die beiden großen Gebäudekomplexe in bester Lage mit neuem Leben erfüllen können, wenn eine teure Renovierung für jeden Investor zum Verlustgeschäft geworden wäre? Hätte man noch viele weitere Jahre, vielleicht Jahrzehnte, dem langsamen Verfall der alten Gemäuer zuschauen sollen? Oder ist es dann nicht vernünftiger, gleich den Abrissbagger zu holen und einen Neubau hinzustellen, der Geschäfte, Arbeitsplätze und Wohnungen in die Innenstadt bringt? Fragen wie diese werden sich wohl auch in der Zukunft bei Baumaßnahmen im Stadtzentrum immer wieder stellen.

Angesichts so mancher Sünden der Vergangenheit wird man von den politisch Verantwortlichen künftig besonderes Fingerspitzengefühl verlangen müssen. Es gilt, achtsam mit dem städtebaulichen Erbe umzugehen und die wenigen noch erhaltenen historischen Gebäude in der Stadt – soweit irgendwie möglich – vor dem Verfall oder Abriss zu bewahren. Die öffentliche Hand müsste privaten Eigentümern von Baudenkmälern bei den enormen Kosten für die Renovierung ihrer historischen Gebäude aber mehr als bisher unter die Arme greifen. Im Einzelfall wäre auch ein stärkeres Engagement der Kommunen – eventuell sogar in der Rolle des Investors – gefordert, um die Renovierung schützenswerter Bausubstanz zu ermöglichen.

Beispiele dafür gibt es in Pfaffenhofen bereits, wie etwa das alte Postamt am unteren Hauptplatz, Ecke Sonnenstraße. Im Jahr 1986 wurde das Gebäude nach dem Umzug der Post in den Neubau am Stadtgraben abgerissen. Nur die 80 Jahre alte Fassade blieb stehen, um das Erscheinungsbild des Hauptplatz-Ensembles zu bewahren. Dahinter errichtete die Stadt entlang der Sonnenstraße ein neues Gebäude, das sich in seiner Gestaltung am Vorgängerbau aus dem Jahr 1908 orientierte. Ähn-

From the neo-Gothic Town Hall on the east side, the square stretches almost 300 metres westwards to the towering Gothic spire of the St Johannes parish church and the community centre. The imposing architecture in the square dates back to the Middle Ages and bears witness to the considerable significance the city had even then as an important administrative centre of the Wittelsbach rulers, and to the prosperity and self-assurance of its inhabitants. The transformation of the square showed the impressive backdrop to much greater advantage than was possible before when tall, canopied chestnut trees and cars parked at all angles dominated the appearance of the street. Today more than ever before, Pfaffenhofen's main square is quite rightly regarded as one of the most beautiful town squares in Upper Bavaria.

The reshaping of the square also served as the initial spark for other forward-looking investments in the city centre, such as the construction of a new commercial and office building on Ingolstädter Strasse, on the long unused Franzbräu and Siglbräu areas of land. The city council's decision to acquire the office space on the upper floors of this new building for the city administration cleared the way for the investor Hans Baierl (Trend Immobilien) to carry out his long-delayed project. To create the necessary additional parking spaces, Baierl took on another major construction work in the city centre in 2010 and 2011: on the grounds of the former Hotel Bortenschlager, which had also lain unused for years on end, between the main square and Auenstrasse, he built attractive sales areas, office premises for an employment agency and job centre, as well as a modern, multi-storey car park with space for 160 vehicles.

However much the new shopping attractions and the revitalization of the city centre may delight Pfaffenhofen's citizens, many of them regret that it came at the expense of the Sigl brewery and the Hotel Bortenschlager, two ancient institutions of tavern culture steeped in history and rich with personal memories but now gone forever from the cityscape. But it would have been impossible to breathe life into both optimally located building complexes if each investor had been saddled with costly renovation work that would turn each business into a loss-making undertaking. Should the planners have spent even more years, possibly decades, watching the old walls slowly fall into further ruin? Wasn't it more reasonable to call in the demolition diggers straightaway and put up a new building that would bring shops and businesses, workplaces and housing into the city centre? Such considerations will remain an issue whenever a city centre faces construction work.

Given some of the sins of the past, forthcoming decisions will demand a great deal of tact on the part of policy makers. They will have to exercise caution when dealing with a city's urban heritage and – wherev-

Beispiel für einen gelungenen Kompromiss zwischen Denkmalschutz und den Erfordernissen einer zeitgemäßen baulichen Nutzung ist das ehemalige Postamt am Hauptplatz. Beim Neubau im Jahr 1986 blieb die historische Fassade aus dem Jahr 1908 erhalten.

The former post office on the main square is a good example of a successful compromise between protecting a historic monument and meeting present-day requirements for its structural use. The original facade from 1908 was preserved when the post office was rebuilt in 1986.

Baukräne beherrschen seit Jahren die Silhouette im Pfaffenhofener Stadtzentrum – Symbol für die dynamische Entwicklung von einer einstmals verschlafenen Kleinstadt zu einem lebendigen Mittelzentrum.

For some years now, the Pfaffenhofen skyline has been dominated by construction cranes – symbolic of the dynamic development of what was once a sleepy little town into a vibrant regional centre.

liche Kompromisslösungen, die sowohl den Belangen des Denkmalschutzes als auch den Erfordernissen einer vernünftigen wirtschaftlichen Nutzung Rechnung trugen, wurden auch bei privaten Projekten wie dem Weilhammer-Anwesen (neben dem Rathaus) und dem alten Gassnerhaus (heute Trendshop) realisiert.

Eine vernünftige Balance zwischen Bewahren und Verändern gilt es auch im innerstädtischen Wohnungsbau zu finden, der sich seit Ende der 2000er Jahre in Pfaffenhofen mit besonderer Dynamik entwickelt. Viele

er possible – safeguard its few remaining historic buildings against decay and demolition. In individual cases, the local community may have to show greater commitment – possibly as an investor itself – if the structural fabric of buildings worthy of protection is to be saved.

The old post office at the lower end of Pfaffenhofen's main square, at the corner of Sonnenstrasse, is one of several examples. In 1986, the building was torn down after the postal service moved to new premises near the *Stadtgraben*. All that was left standing was the 80-year-old fa-

Unterer Hauptplatz und Rathaus vom Turm der Stadtpfarrkirche aus fotografiert.
Lower end of the main square and the town hall photographed from the parish church.

zentrumsnahe Siedlungsgebiete, deren Bausubstanz überwiegend noch aus der ersten Hälfte des vergangenen Jahrhunderts stammte oder teilweise noch älter war, haben ihren ursprünglichen Charakter schon längst verändert. Kleine Vorstadthäuser mit idyllischen Vorgärten, Bäumen, Blumen und Gemüsebeeten sind durch große Wohnkomplexe verdrängt worden. Die Kommunalpolitik wird darauf achten müssen, den in manchen Quartieren zu beobachtenden städtebaulichen Wildwuchs einzudämmen. Gerade in Zeiten einer wahren Goldgräberstimmung im gewerblichen Wohnungsbau braucht die Stadt neue Konzepte für eine Architektur, die nicht nur an maximaler Raumnutzung und Rendite ausgerichtet ist. Davon wird abhängen, welches städtebauliche Erbe wir unseren Nachfahren hinterlassen. Uniforme, seelenlose Wohn- und Büromaschinen aus Glas und Beton oder Häuser, die trotz einer modernen architektonischen Handschrift auch noch ein Stück Pfaffenhofener Identität und Tradition erkennen lassen. Die jüngst in der Öffentlichkeit diskutierte Idee, bei der Planung von Neubauprojekten in sensiblen Altstadtbereichen einen Gestaltungsbeirat einzubeziehen, könnte ein Schritt in die richtige Richtung sein.

Bei allem Bedauern, dass so manche idyllische Winkel, vertraute Gebäude und Plätze der alten Stadtheimat nur noch in romantischen Erinnerungen und historischen Bildern weiterleben, wird aber an einer intensiveren baulichen Nutzung der innerstädtischen Flächen kein Weg vorbeiführen. Nur auf diese Weise lässt sich der zunehmende Flächenverbrauch in der freien Natur eindämmen. Als Modellkommune im Programm „Flächenressourcen-Management" des Freistaates Bayern verfolgt die Stadt Pfaffenhofen schon seit einiger Zeit die Strategie, ungenutzte Flächen im Zentrum zu reaktivieren. Wie zum Beispiel das Gelände der ehemaligen Zahnradfabrik Herion. Das 20 000 qm große Areal, nur fünf Gehminuten vom Hauptplatz entfernt, lag nach der Schließung des Werkes viele Jahre lang brach. Jetzt gibt es hier eine Sozialstation sowie zentrumsnahen Wohnraum für 350 Menschen, was eine Einsparung von etwa sechs Hektar Fläche im Umland bedeutet.

cade, so as to preserve the overall appearance of the ensemble of buildings. The design of the new building that went up behind it on Sonnenstrasse was based on its predecessor, built in 1908. Similar compromise solutions taking into account the protection of historic buildings and the requirements of economic viability were also adopted for privately funded projects, such as the Weilhammer property (next to the town hall) and the old Gassner house (now the Trendshop).

A reasonable balance between preservation and change must also be found for inner-city housing construction, which has been especially dynamic in Pfaffenhofen since the end of the last decade. Many of the settlements located close to the city centre and whose structural fabric dated back mostly to the first half of the 1900s have long since lost their original character: the small suburban houses with idyllic front gardens, trees, flowers and vegetable patches have been replaced by large residential complexes. Local politicians will have to find ways to curb the rank urban growth that can be observed in some areas. When the prevailing mood in commercial housing construction is a "gold-digging mentality", what the city needs is new architectural concepts that focus on more than just the maximum utilization of available space and income return. This will determine the kind of urban heritage we pass on to our children: uniform, soulless residential machines and offices of concrete and glass, or houses that, while reflecting a modern architectural signature, retain something of Pfaffenhofen's identity and traditions. The recently discussed idea of involving an architectural advisory committee in any new building project planned in sensitive old town areas may be a step in the right direction.

Regretful as it may be that many of the old home town's idyllic little nooks, familiar buildings and squares now live on only in romantic reminiscences and historical images, there's no alternative to a more intensive use of buildings in inner-city spaces. This is the only way of keeping increasing land consumption in the countryside under control. As a model community within the framework of Bavaria's programme for the

Zudem konnte die Stadt eine der alten Werkhallen erwerben und mit relativ bescheidenen Mitteln zu einem Kulturzentrum umgestalten. So ist es der Kommune nun möglich, in Zusammenarbeit mit dem neuen Pfaffenhofener Kunstverein hochkarätige Ausstellungen in die Kreisstadt zu holen, die beim Publikum und in den Medien überregionale Beachtung finden, wie etwa eine große Beuys-Schau im Sommer 2011.

Die Kulturhalle, aber auch Straßen und Plätze, der Festsaal im alten Rathaus, die Schulturnhallen, die Kirchen und das Haus der Begegnung bieten das ganze Jahr über die Bühnen für eine Vielzahl von Ausstellungen, Konzerten, Lesungen, Kabarett- und Theateraufführungen. Glanzpunkte setzt alljährlich der Pfaffenhofener Kultursommer mit jeweils rund 40 Einzelveranstaltungen. Nicht zu vergessen Wacky Singers Künstlerwerkstatt, ein Mekka der Jazzfans, in dem sich Newcomer aber auch Topstars der Szene ein Stelldichein geben. Die städtische Musikschule, die Stadtkapelle und mehrere private Institute bieten vielfältige Möglichkeiten, ein Instrument, das Singen oder Tanzen zu erlernen. Auch die alternative junge Kunstszene hat in Pfaffenhofen ihren Platz. Graffiti-Sprüher nutzen mit Erlaubnis der Stadt Betonwände und alte Gemäuer im öffentlichen Raum für ihre Kreativität. Die Musik-Initiative der Stadtjugendpflege gibt jungen Talenten die Chance, öffentlich aufzutreten, zum Beispiel beim jährlichen Saitensprung-Openair-Festival.

Wer es lieber traditionell und bodenständig mag, der findet in Pfaffenhofen bei Volkstanz, Stubenmusik und Mundartlesungen ein vielfältiges Veranstaltungsangebot. In der Schule und im Kindergarten wird noch der oberbayerische Dialekt gesprochen. Und mit Dirndl, Lederhose, Trachtenhut und Lodenjanker sieht man die Pfaffenhofener nicht nur beim Volksfest im September oder beim Volksmusik-Hoagart, sondern auch das ganze Jahr über bei festlichen Anlässen genauso wie werktags im Biergarten.

Bei allem Traditionsbewusstsein sind die Pfaffenhofener aber auch weltoffen und tolerant, wobei es **den** typischen Pfaffenhofener eigentlich gar nicht gibt, wenn man bedenkt, dass sich die Einwohnerzahl der Stadt seit Anfang der 1970er Jahre mehr als verdoppelt hat. Viele Zugezogene aus dem In- und Ausland haben an der Ilm eine neue Heimat gefunden und wie in anderen Wachstumsregionen auch, hat sich in Pfaffenhofen ein bunter Mix aus unterschiedlichen Kulturen und Nationalitäten über Jahrzehnte hinweg im toleranten Miteinander zu einem lebendigen Gemeinwesen zusammengefunden.

Aus vielen ehemaligen „Gastarbeitern“ türkischer, italienischer, griechischer oder anderer Herkunft sind heute voll integrierte Stadtbürger geworden. Anfang des Jahres 2012 lebten rund 2100 Migranten (knapp 9 Prozent der Bevölkerung) aus über 80 Ländern in der Kreisstadt.

Toleranz und Integration werden in Pfaffenhofen groß geschrieben. Bei vielen Veranstaltungen ist es guter Brauch, dass Alt- und Neubürger aus unterschiedlichen Kulturkreisen und Religionen gemeinsam feiern.
Tolerance and integration are a major priority in Pfaffenhofen. It has become a tradition at many events to invite old and new inhabitants from different cultural backgrounds and religions to celebrate together.

management of vacant buildings and open land, Pfaffenhofen has for some time now been following the strategy of reactivating unused areas in the city centre, such as the grounds of the former Herion cog factory. The 20,000-square-metre area, just five minutes on foot from the main square, was left unused for many years after the factory closed down. Now, a social centre and living space for 350 people is being built near the city centre, which will save roughly six hectares of land in the surrounding area.

The city was also able to acquire an old factory hall and convert it with relatively modest means into a cultural centre. This enabled the local community to join forces with the Pfaffenhofen Art Society in bringing to the city the kind of high-quality exhibitions that gain the nationwide interest of both the public and the media – such as the major Joseph Beuys exhibition in the summer of 2011.

Throughout the year, the city's arts and cultural centre, its streets and squares, the banqueting hall at the old town hall, school gymnasiums, its churches and the community centre all serve as venues for a wide range of exhibitions, public readings, cabaret evenings and theatrical performances. The annual highlights are provided by Pfaffenhofen's Cultural Summer Programme with its 40 or so individual events, not to

Wenn in Pfaffenhofen gefeiert wird – und Anlässe dafür gibt es im Lauf des Jahres sehr viele – dann ist die Stadtkapelle immer mit dabei.
Whenever there's a celebration in Pfaffenhofen – and there are many such occasions over the years – the town band always has a part to play.

Pfaffenhofen ist ein Zentrum des Hallertauer Hopfenanbaus. Das „grüne Gold", das auf den Hügeln rund um die Kreisstadt wächst, prägt schon seit dem 19. Jahrhundert die Landschaft und die Menschen in der Region.

Pfaffenhofen is a centre of hop production in the Hallertau region. The "green gold" that grows on the hills surrounding the district capital has been a defining feature of the region's landscape and its people since the 19th century.

Als Beispiel für ein funktionierendes Miteinander haben die interkulturellen und interreligiösen Wochen einen festen Platz im Veranstaltungskalender der Stadt. Auf Initiative der katholischen Kirchengemeinde und des Internationalen Kulturvereins Pfaffenhofen finden sich hier Bürger der unterschiedlichen Nationalitäten und Religionen zusammen, um sich besser kennen zu lernen. Es ist in Pfaffenhofen schon lange guter Brauch, dass bei besonderen Ereignissen und Festen auch Gruppen aus anderen Kulturkreisen und Religionsgemeinschaften in die Programmgestaltung einbezogen werden.

Über den eigenen Kirchturm hinauszuschauen und neuen Ideen offen zu begegnen, hat in Pfaffenhofen eine lange Tradition. Wohl auch durch den hier schon seit etwa 200 Jahren verbreiteten Hopfenanbau. Weil sie das „grüne Gold" nicht nur für den regionalen Bedarf produzierten, sondern in alle Welt verkauften, standen die Landwirte in der Hallertau neuen Märkten und technischen Innovationen immer schon aufgeschlossen gegenüber. Der Anschluss an die Bahnlinie München-Nürnberg (1867) und die Hallertauer Lokalbahn von Rohrbach in Richtung Mainburg sorgten nicht nur für ideale Möglichkeiten zum Transport der landwirtschaftlichen Güter. Auch Handwerker, Gewerbetreibende und kleine Industriebetriebe nutzten die neuen Chancen, ihre Produkte überregional im In- und Ausland zu vermarkten. Dass Pfaffenhofen als eine der ersten Kleinstädte Bayerns schon Ende des 19. Jahrhunderts eine öffentliche Stromversorgung erhielt und hier mit einem Dampfkraftwerk der Grundstein der späteren Isar-Amperwerke (heute aufgegangen im E.ON-Konzern) gelegt wurde, förderte ebenfalls die Entwicklung der Stadt zu einem prosperierenden Wirtschaftsstandort.

Den Namen Pfaffenhofen international bekannt gemacht hat vor allem der Babynahrungshersteller Hipp. Dem weltweit größten Verarbeiter von Rohstoffen aus biologischer Erzeugung verdankt Pfaffenhofen auch seinen überregionalen Ruf als Vorzeigestadt in Sachen Ökologie und Nachhaltigkeit. Ein weiteres ökologisches Aushängeschild ist das Biomasse-Heizkraftwerk, mit dem die Kreisstadt als erste Kommune in ganz Deutschland bereits im Jahr 2001 die Klimaschutz-Vorgaben des Kyoto-Protokolls erfüllen konnte.

Das nachhaltige Siedlungskonzept Ecoquartier auf dem Kramerbräu-Gelände im Ortsteil Weihern soll den guten Ruf der Stadt als Zentrum für Ökologie und grüne Technologien weiter untermauern. Dort werden Wohnungen für 450 Menschen sowie ein Kompetenzzentrum mit ökologisch orientierten Unternehmen ausschließlich mit nachhaltig unbedenklichen Materialien errichtet und aus regenerativen Energiequellen versorgt.

mention Wacky Singers Künstlerwerkstatt, a mecca for jazz fans and a gathering place for jazz newcomers and stars. The municipal music school, the town band and several private institutes offer ample opportunities for people to learn to play an instrument, sing and dance. The young alternative art scene also has its place in Pfaffenhofen: graffiti sprayers have permission from the city authorities to use concrete walls and old masonry in public places to give free rein to their creativity. The music initiative started by the city's youth welfare office gives talented young people a chance to perform in public, such as at the annual *Saitensprung* open-air festival.

Those who prefer things a little more traditional and down-to-earth will find a varied programme of events in Pfaffenhofen's offerings of folk dances, folk music and readings in the regional dialect – the Upper Bavarian dialect is still spoken in schools and kindergartens. And it's not only at the September Festival or the *Volksmusik-Hoagart* concerts that Pfaffenhofen locals wear their traditional hats, bonnets, dirndls, lederhosen and loden jackets: they also wear them on festive occasions throughout the year as well as in beer gardens during the week.

For all their sense of tradition, Pfaffenhofen's inhabitants are also open-minded and tolerant, although in reality there's no such thing as a typical *Pfaffenhofener*, as the city's population has more than doubled since the early 1970s. Many newcomers from other parts of Germany and abroad have found a new home here on the River Ilm – and as in other growth regions, too, a colourful mix of different cultures and nationalities has congregated here in a spirit of tolerant coexistence over a period of decades to form a lively local community.

Many former *Gastarbeiter* of Turkish, Italian, Greek or other origin are today fully integrated citizens of Pfaffenhofen. At the beginning of 2012, this district capital had about 2,100 immigrants (almost nine per cent of the population) from 80 countries.

The intercultural and interreligious weeks – an initiative of the Catholic parish and Pfaffenhofen's International Cultural Association – are a permanent fixture on the city's calendar of events and provide a good example of functioning coexistence. At these events, local citizens of different nationalities and religions gather to get to know each other better. Pfaffenhofen has established a good custom of involving groups from other cultural circles and religious communities in the organization of special events and celebrations.

Pfaffenhofen has a long tradition of looking beyond its own church tower and remaining receptive to new ideas. This open-mindedness is probably due in part to the region's roughly 200-year history of cultivating hops. This "green gold" wasn't produced to meet regional needs

Am Hauptplatz gibt es eine kostenlose Tankstelle für Elektrofahrzeuge und der Strom für die städtischen Liegenschaften wird zu 100 Prozent aus Wasserkraft gewonnen. Einen weiteren Schritt zur grünen Vorzeigekommune macht die Stadt mit der Ausrichtung der kleinen Landesgartenschau „Natur in Pfaffenhofen an der Ilm" im Jahr 2017. Ziel ist es unter anderem, die Ilmufer im innerstädtischen Bereich ökologisch aufzuwerten und den Fluss auch als Erlebnisraum für die Bürger zu erschließen.

Was Pfaffenhofen für viele Menschen so lebens- und liebenswert macht, sind nicht nur die perfekte Infrastruktur mit optimaler medizinischer und sozialer Versorgung, einem breit gefächerten Bildungsangebot, modernen Freizeiteinrichtungen sowie attraktiven Geschäften und Gastronomiebetrieben. Vorbildlich sind in der Stadt auch die vielfältigen Möglichkeiten des Bürgerdialogs und der aktiven Mitgestaltung. Mit dem nach der Kommunalwahl 2008 installierten Aktionsprogramm „PAF und DU" haben Bürgermeister Thomas Herker, der Stadtrat und die Verwaltung völlig neue Wege der Bürgerbeteiligung eröffnet. Über Internetportale, aber auch in offenen Arbeitskreisen und Workshops können alle Stadtbewohner, Vereine und Verbände ihre Ideen, Wünsche, Anregungen und Kritik einbringen. Bei wichtigen kommunalen Projekten werden die Bürger von Politik und Verwaltung aktiv in die Entscheidungsfindung mit einbezogen. So konnten die Pfaffenhofener bei der Neugestaltung des Hauptplatzes über viele Details wie die Auswahl der Parkbänke oder die Gestaltung der Brunnen mitentscheiden.

In Pfaffenhofen zeigt sich, dass das Zusammenleben zwischen Alt und Jung nicht nur in der Familie, sondern auch in einem lebendigen Gemeinwesen funktionieren kann. Zum Beispiel wenn junge Leute den älteren im Seniorenbüro erklären, wie man das Smartphone bedient, oder rüstige Senioren sich als Fahrer für die Rufbusse der Linie Nacht engagieren, mit der Jugendliche am Wochenende sicher von der Party oder der Disco nach Hause fahren können. Weitere vorbildliche Einrichtungen der städtischen Jugendarbeit sind ein aktives Jugendparlament, das multimediale Kreativzentrum Utopia und das Projekt Studioladen, das jungen Menschen mit innovativen Ideen ermöglicht, ohne größeres finanzielles Risiko den Schritt in die Selbstständigkeit zu testen.

In Pfaffenhofen werden auch die Menschen nicht vergessen, die wegen Krankheiten oder anderer unglücklicher Umstände in finanzielle Probleme geraten sind oder ein so geringes Einkommen haben, dass sie an der Armutsgrenze leben müssen. Um diese Menschen kümmern sich zahlreiche soziale Verbände und Gruppen wie die Pfaffenhofener Tafel, die Caritas oder der Verein Familien in Not. Die Stadt unterstützt sie mit Sozialrabatten in öffentlichen Einrichtungen wie dem städtischen Frei-

alone, but was sold all over the world, so local farmers in the Hallertau region have always been open to new markets and technical innovations. Linking up to the Munich-to-Nuremberg railway line in 1867 and the local Hallertau railway from Rohrbach to Mainburg did more than ensure ideal possibilities for transporting agricultural goods. Craftsmen, tradesmen and small industrial enterprises took advantage of these new opportunities to market their products nationwide and abroad. In the late 1890s, Pfaffenhofen became one of the first small towns in Bavaria to get a public electricity supply. This, together with a steam-generating power station, laid the foundation for what was to become the regional energy supplier Isar-Amperwerke (now part of the E.ON Group). It also helped the town develop into a prospering business location.

The name "Pfaffenhofen" is known internationally mainly because of the baby food manufacturer Hipp, the world's largest processor of organically farmed produce. The city also has Hipp to thank for its nationwide reputation as a flagship with regard to ecology and sustainability. Another ecological showpiece is the biomass-fuelled combined heat and power plant, with which, as early as 2001, Pfaffenhofen became the first local community in Germany to comply with the Kyoto Protocol's requirements for climate protection.

Ecoquartier, the sustainable housing concept on the Kramerbräu grounds, is intended to underscore Pfaffenhofen's reputation as a centre of ecology and green technology. Here, in the Weihern district of the city, homes are being built for 450 people, along with a centre of competence comprising ecologically oriented companies. The construction materials used are all environmentally safe and the buildings will be supplied with renewable energy sources.

At the main square, electric vehicles can be recharged for free, and the electricity for municipal properties is entirely hydropower-generated. In keeping with its role as an exemplary green community, the city will be hosting the small state garden show "Nature in Pfaffenhofen an der Ilm" in 2017. One of its goals is to ecologically upgrade the banks of the River Ilm within the city and to make the river accessible as an adventure sphere.

A perfect infrastructure with optimal medical and social care, a wide range of educational opportunities, modern leisure facilities and attractive shops and restaurants are just some of the things that make Pfaffenhofen so liveable and loveable. Equally important, however, are the many opportunities its citizens have to engage in civic dialogue and active involvement. With the "PAF and YOU" programme of action initiated after the 2008 local elections, Mayor Thomas Herker, the city council and the municipal administration have added an entirely new dimension to civic participation. It enables all Pfaffenhofen citizens, clubs and associations

Blick von der Burgfriedenstraße Richtung Westen: Eindrucksvoll überragt die Pfarrkirche St. Johannes Baptist die Innenstadt. Links der Rathausturm.
Westward view from Burgfriedenstrasse, with the parish church of St Johannes Baptist towering impressively above the city centre. To the left, the town hall tower.

bad oder Gebührenermäßigungen für die Kinderbetreuung. Für die Ärmsten der Armen unterhält die Stadt ein modernes Gebäude mit menschenwürdigem Wohnraum für Obdachlose.

Sportbegeisterte finden in Pfaffenhofen ein großes Angebot, ihre Freizeit aktiv zu gestalten. Über 60 Vereine bieten vielfältige Möglichkeiten von der Gymnastik bis zum Segelfliegen. Ein modernes Warmfreibad mit Sprungturm, 50-Meter- und Erlebnisbecken, mehrere moderne Mehrzweckhallen, Beachvolleyball- und Tennisanlagen, Rasen- und Streetsoccerplätze für die Fußballer, die 13 Meter hohe Kletterhalle des Alpenvereins, ein Kunsteisstadion sowie mehrere Fitness-Studios bieten Freizeitspaß das ganze Jahr über. Auch junge Trendsportarten haben in Pfaffenhofen einen guten Boden. Allen voran die Skateboarder, denen die Stadt im Untergeschoss der Kulturhalle auf dem alten Heriongelände

to contribute ideas and suggestions, make requests and express criticism via Internet portals, as well as in open work groups and workshops. When it comes to important municipal projects, politicians and administrative officials actively involve the city's inhabitants in the decision-making process. This was how locals came to have a say in many of the details concerning the restyling of the main square, such as the choice of park benches and the design of the fountain. And since 2012, all city council sessions have been streamed live on the Internet.

Pfaffenhofen has shown that old and young people can live side by side not only within a family, but also in a vibrant local community. Take, for example, the young people at the senior citizens' bureau who show the elderly how to use a Smartphone, or the sprightly pensioners who drive the on-call buses at night that make sure youngsters get home safely from their weekend party or disco visit. Other commendable institutions in urban youth work are an active Youth Parliament, the multimedia creative centre Utopia, and the Studioladen project, which enables young people with innovative ideas to take their first steps towards self-employment without any major financial risk.

But Pfaffenhofen also has a heart for those of its citizens who are in financial difficulty through illness or other unfortunate circumstances, or who have such small incomes that they live close to the poverty line. Taking care of these people are many social organizations and groups, such as the Pfaffenhofen food bank, Caritas, and the Families in Need Association. The city provides support in the form of social discounts for public facilities, like the municipal swimming pool, and reductions in fees for childcare. And for the poorest of the poor, the city maintains a modern building that provides decent housing for homeless people.

Sports enthusiasts in Pfaffenhofen have a broad range of leisure activities to choose from, with more than 60 clubs offering a variety of opportunies for recreation and sport, from gymnastics to gliding. A modern, outdoor, heated swimming pool with a diving platform, a 50-metre pool and an adventure pool, several modern multi-purpose halls, beach volleyball and tennis courts, grass pitches and street soccer courts for footballers, a 13-metre-high climbing hall owned by the Alpine Association, an ice stadium, as well as several fitness studios provide leisure fun all year round. Pfaffenhofen is also good for young trend sports, and for skateboarders in particular: on the basement floor of the cultural centre, on the grounds of the former Herion factory, the city has put at their disposal the largest indoor fun-sports arena in Bavaria.

For those who prefer to spend their free time out in the open, there are ideal opportunities only minutes away from the city centre for people to go jogging, Nordic walking or just take a stroll. There are marked

die größte Indoor-Funsportarena Bayerns zur Verfügung gestellt hat.

Wer seine Freizeit lieber draußen in der freien Natur verbringt, findet nur wenige Minuten vom Stadtzentrum entfernt ideale Möglichkeiten zum Joggen, Nordic Walken oder ganz einfach zum Spazierengehen. In den Wäldern im Westen und Osten der Stadt gibt es markierte Wanderwege und einen Fitnessparcours. Auch für Mountainbiker und Radwanderer ist die Umgebung der Kreisstadt ein abwechslungsreiches und landschaftlich überaus reizvolles Revier. Zahlreiche markierte Routen führen durch Pfaffenhofen und verbinden die Kreisstadt mit dem überregionalen Streckennetz, wie etwa dem Donau-, dem Paar- und dem Isar-Radwanderweg.

Die Hügellandschaft rund um die Kreisstadt wird geprägt durch die sechs Meter hohen Gerüstanlagen der Hopfengärten. 600 000 Zentner des grünen Goldes wurden im Jahr 2011 in der Hallertau, dem weltgrößten geschlossenen Anbaugebiet, geerntet. Wer während der Erntezeit durch die ländlichen Ortsteile der Stadt fährt, kann hier das grüne Gold mit allen Sinnen erleben, wenn die Hopfendarren surren und die Ventilatoren das würzige Dolden-Aroma über die Dörfer verbreiten.

Ganz besondere Düfte kann man in Pfaffenhofen auch bei einem Besuch in der ältesten Wachszieherei und Lebzelterei Deutschlands schnuppern. Seit über 400 Jahren werden im Café Hipp am Hauptplatz Votivgaben aus Wachs und mit Bienenhonig gesüßte Lebzelten hergestellt.

Und in der unmittelbaren Nachbarschaft oder weniger als eine Autostunde entfernt, erreicht man von Pfaffenhofen aus neben den zahlreichen Kulturstätten, Museen und historischen Sehenswürdigkeiten in der Landeshauptstadt München noch viele weitere Ausflugsziele und touristische Attraktionen wie das Hopfenmuseum in Wolnzach, das Kelten- und Römermuseum in Manching, das Benediktinerkloster Scheyern, den Waldkletterpark bei Jetzendorf, das Bayerische Armeemuseum, das Landesgartenschaugelände und das Audi-Forum in Ingolstadt, die Thermen in Erding, Bad Gögging und Bad Abbach, den Donaudurchbruch zwischen Kloster Weltenburg und Kelheim, Regensburg mit seinem prächtigen Dom, Eichstätt im Naturpark Altmühltal oder auch die Bischofsstadt Freising mit dem legendären Biergarten der Brauerei Weihenstephan. Und auch die Fugger-Stadt Augsburg ist in weniger als einer Stunde erreichbar. Golfer finden in Reichertshausen und Gerolsbach zwei 18-Loch-Plätze in unmittelbarer Nachbarschaft der Kreisstadt und viele weitere in den angrenzenden Landkreisen.

Aber es gibt noch sehr viel mehr zu entdecken in der lebens- und liebenswerten Kreisstadt an der Ilm und ihrer reizvollen Umgebung. Die folgenden Seiten sollen dazu einladen.

hiking trails and a fitness course in the woods in the east and the west of the city, and the beautiful and varied landscape surrounding the city is ideal territory for mountain bikers and cycle hikers. Numerous marked routes lead through the city, connecting it with the national route network, such as the Donau, Paar and Isar cycle tracks.

A distinct feature of the rolling hills around the city are the six-metre-high trellises of the hop gardens. The Hallertau region is the world's largest hop-growing area and it harvested 600,000 tons of the green gold in 2011. Anyone driving through the rural parts of the city during harvest time will experience the green gold in different ways as the oast houses, or hop kilns, hum and whirr and the ventilators fan the fruity aroma of the drying hop cones over the villages.

Other special fragrances in Pfaffenhofen can be experienced on a visit to Germany's oldest candle-making workshop and gingerbread bakery. Café Hipp on the main square has been producing wax votive offerings and gingerbread sweetened with natural honey for more than 400 years.

In addition to the numerous cultural and historic sites and museums in the City of Munich, less than an hour's drive from Pfaffenhofen and its immediate vicinity, there are a great many other excursion destinations and tourist attractions. These include: the German Hop Museum in Wolnzach, the Celtic-Roman Museum in Manching, the Benedictine monastery in Scheyern, the climbing park in the forest near Jetzendorf, the Bavarian Army Museum, the state garden exhibition area and the Audi-Forum in Ingolstadt, the thermal baths in Erding, Bad Gögging and Bad Abbach, the Danube breakthrough between Weltenburg monastery and Kelheim, Regensburg with its magnificent cathedral, the Baroque city of Eichstätt in the Altmühltal Nature Park, and the episcopal city of Freising with the legendary beer garden of the Weihenstephan brewery. Augsburg, the home of the Fugger family, can also be reached within an hour. Also in the immediate vicinity are two 18-hole golfing greens, in Reichertshausen and Gerolsbach, and many more in the neighbouring districts.

But there is still very much more to be discovered in the most liveable and loveable city on the Ilm and its beautiful surroundings. The following pages invite you to take a look.

Blick über den Marienbrunnen auf den oberen Hauptplatz. Wer das pulsierende Zentrum der Stadt fast autofrei und menschenleer erleben möchte, muss an einem Sonntagmorgen früh aufstehen.
View across the Marian fountain onto the upper end of the main square. To see the pulsating town centre deserted and almost free of cars, you have to get up very early on a Sunday morning.

5 PFAFFENHOFENER KALEIDOSKOP
PFAFFENHOFEN KALEIDOSCOPE

5.1 SEHENSWÜRDIGKEITEN, STRASSEN UND PLÄTZE

Die Pfarrkirche St. Johannes Baptist ist das bauliche Wahrzeichen der Stadt Pfaffenhofen. Der in drei Etagen sich verjüngende Turm ragt mit seiner schlanken Kupferspitze und dem vergoldeten Kreuz genau 77,71 Meter über den Hauptplatz und prägt von weitem das Bild der Kreisstadt. Nach dem Katastrophenjahr 1388, als der Markt samt der romanischen Vorgängerkirche im Städtekrieg zwischen den Wittelsbacher Landesfürsten und dem Bund der Reichsstädte niedergebrannt worden war, bauten die Pfaffenhofener die neue dreischiffige Basilika im spätgotischen Stil. 1409 war das Werk vollendet. In der zweiten Hälfte des 17. Jahrhunderts wurde der Innenraum im Barockstil neu gestaltet.
Wegen der stark gestiegenen Einwohnerzahl ließ der damalige Pfarrer Ludwig Kohnle im Jahr 1913 das Langhaus der Stadtpfarrkirche um zwei Joche nach Westen verlängern. Seither ist das Gotteshaus in seiner äußeren Gestalt weitgehend unverändert geblieben, wurde aber mehrfach aufwändig renoviert.

PLACES OF INTEREST, STREETS AND SQUARES

The parish church of St Johannes Baptist is Pfaffenhofen's structural landmark. The tower tapers upwards in three tiers, ending in a slender copper tip and a gilded cross exactly 77.71 metres above the main square, and lending the district capital its character, even from afar. After the catastrophe year of 1388, when the market and the Romanesque church that stood here were burned to the ground during the city war between the local Wittelsbach rulers and the alliance of imperial cities, Pfaffenhofen built its new, three-aisled basilica in the late-Gothic style, completing construction in 1409. In the second half of the 17th century, the church interior was reworked in the Baroque style.
In 1913, to accommodate the sharp rise in the population, the parish priest at the time, Ludwig Kohnle, had the nave of the church extended to the west by two bays. The outer appearance of this house of worship has remained virtually unchanged ever since, although the interior has been fully renovated several times.

Die Mariengrotte im Turm der Stadtpfarrkirche St. Johannes Baptist wurde 1888 von August Dirigl gestaltet, einem angesehenen Landschaftsplastiker, der auch für den Märchenkönig Ludwig II. in Schloss Linderhof arbeitete. Auch heute noch wird die Grotte, die dem Gnadenort Lourdes nachempfunden ist, von vielen Pfaffenhofenern zum Gebet und zur stillen Einkehr genutzt.

The Marian grotto in the tower of the parish church of St. Johannes Baptist was designed in 1888 by August Dirigl, a respected landscape sculptor who also worked for the fairy-tale king Ludwig II at Linderhof Castle. The grotto, which is based on the place of grace at Lourdes, is used to this day by many Pfaffenhofen parishioners as a place of prayer and quiet contemplation.

ie Stadtpfarrkirche mit ihrer prächtigen Barockausstattung dient der katholischen emeinde nicht nur als Raum für Gottesdienste und andere religiöse Feiern, sondern uch als festliche Kulisse für Konzerte.

/ith its magnificent Baroque interior, the parish church serves the Catholic parish ɔt only as a space for worship and other religious ceremonies, but also as a festive ackdrop for concerts.

Die Krönung Mariens. Diese gotische Holzplastik (um 1480) gehört zu den ältesten Kunstschätzen der Stadtpfarrkirche.

The coronation of the Virgin Mary. This Gothic wooden statue (circa 1480) is one of the oldest art treasures in the parish church.

Die Spitalkirche wurde zwischen 1716 und 1719 direkt gegenüber der Stadtpfarrkirche an der Nordseite des oberen Hauptplatzes errichtet. Sie diente ursprünglich als Gotteshaus des Franziskanerordens, der hier bis 1802 ein Kloster unterhielt. Ursprünglich befand sich der – wesentlich niedrigere – Glockenturm der Klosterkirche auf der Nordseite des Gebäudes. Er musste aber im Jahr 1900 wegen Baufälligkeit abgetragen werden und wurde durch einen neuen, höheren Turm mit Zwiebelhaube auf der Hauptplatzseite ersetzt. Nach der Säkularisation nutzte die Stadt Pfaffenhofen das aufgelöste Kloster zunächst als Krankenhaus, später als Altenheim. Die Deckenfresken in der Kirche mit Szenen aus dem Leben des Heiligen Franziskus stammen von dem Pfaffenhofener Kirchenmaler Michael P. Weingartner († 1996). In der Weihnachtszeit ist die 200 Jahre alte Krippe mit wechselnden szenischen Darstellungen aus dem Leben der Heiligen Familie ein Anziehungspunkt für Besucher aus nah und fern.

The hospital church was built between 1716 and 1719 directly opposite the parish church, on the north side of the upper part of the main square. It originally served as a place of worship for the Franciscan order, which maintained a monastery here until 1802.

The much lower bell tower of the monastery church was originally located on the north side of the building, but it had to be demolished in 1900 because of its dilapidated condition and it was replaced by a new, taller tower with an onion dome on the side facing the main square. After secularization, Pfaffenhofen used the dissolved monastery first as a hospital, and later as an old people's home. The ceiling frescos in the church depicting scenes from the life of St Francis are by the Pfaffenhofen church painter Michael P. Weingartner († 1996). Every Christmas, the 200-year-old nativity manger and the changing scenic depictions from the life of the Holy Family attract visitors from near and far.

ie evangelische Kreuzkirche wurde im Jahr 1925 an der Einmündung der Moosburger in die Münche-
er Straße errichtet. Bis zu diesem Zeitpunkt stand der zunächst noch sehr kleinen lutherischen Ge-
einschaft für Gottesdienste nur der Pfaffenhofener Rathaussaal zur Verfügung. Mit der steigenden
ıhl evangelischer Zuzügler wuchs auch der Wunsch nach einem eigenen Gotteshaus. Nach dem Kauf
s Grundstückes, auf dem die Stadt früher ein Spital betrieben hatte, konnte das Projekt schließlich
Angriff genommen werden. Bemerkenswert im Innenraum der Kreuzkirche sind die Holzkonstruk-
on des Tonnengewölbes sowie die Wandfresken mit Darstellungen von Geburt, Kreuzigung und Aufer-
ehung Jesu Christi, die 1926 von dem in Nürnberg geborenen Maler Hans Röhm geschaffen wurden.

The Protestant Church of the Holy Cross was built in 1925 at the point where Moosburger Strasse meets Münchener Strasse. Until then, the only meeting place Pfaffenhofen's still very small Lutheran congregation had at its disposal for religious services was the council chamber at the town hall. As the number of Protestant newcomers increased, so did their desire for a church of their own. After purchasing the plot of land on which the city had previously run a hospital, it was possible to finally make a start on the building. Remarkable interior features of the Church of the Holy Cross are the wooden construction of the barrel vault, and the murals – painted in 1926 by the Nuremberg-born artist Hans Röhm – depicting Christ's birth, crucifixion and resurrection.

Seit 1863 steht die Mariensäule in der Mitte des Hauptplatzes. Ursprünglich von einer Grünanlage mit Trauerweiden und zwei kleinen Trinkwasserbrunnen eingerahmt, wurde die Anlage 1964 durch ein Betonbecken mit Springbrunnen ersetzt, ehe sie beim Umbau des Hauptplatzes (2009) ihre jetzige Gestalt erhielt. Die Sandsteinsäule mit der restaurierten Marienstatue aus Bronze thront nun in einem Granit umrandeten Brunnenbecken und ist an schönen Sommertagen ein bevorzugter Treffpunkt der Pfaffenhofener Jugend.

The Marian column has stood at the centre of the main square since 1863. Originally framed by a green space with weeping willows and two small drinking fountains, the area was replaced in 1964 by a concrete basin and fountain before taking on its present appearance during the reconstruction of the main square in 2009. The restored bronze statue of the Virgin Mary now stands atop a sandstone column in a fountain basin clad in granite, and is a favoured meeting place for young people on fine summer days.

Das Ritterhaus am oberen Hauptplatz geht in seinen Ursprüngen auf das 16. Jahrhundert zurück und gehört zu den ältesten und historisch interessantesten Gebäuden im Stadtzentrum. Die prächtige Neubarock-Fassade mit feiner Stuckgliederung und dem Relief der Muttergottes mit Jesuskind über dem Eingangsportal stammt aus der zweiten Hälfte des 19. Jahrhunderts. Ursprünglich war das stattliche Gebäude Amtssitz der Richter und Pfleger, die sich im Dienst der Wittelsbacher Landesfürsten um Rechtsprechung und Verwaltungsgeschäfte im Bezirk Pfaffenhofen kümmerten.

The origins of the *Ritterhaus* at the upper end of the main square go back to the 16th century. It's one of the oldest and historically most interesting buildings in the city centre. The splendid neo-Baroque facade – with its fine stucco outlines and the relief of the Madonna and Child above the entrance portal – dates from the second half of the 19th century. This stately building was originally the official residence of the magistrates and guardians in the service of the local Wittelsbach rulers who saw to the dispensation of justice and day-to-day administration in the Pfaffenhofen district.

Architektonische Akzente setzen am oberen Hauptplatz zwischen Pfarr- und Spitalkirche das idyllische Türmchen über dem Eingang zum ehemaligen Müllerbräukeller-Saal, bis zum 2. Weltkrieg eine Pfaffenhofener Veranstaltungs-Hochburg (großes Foto links), und das Verwaltungsgebäude der Brauerei Müllerbräu (1890/91) mit seiner prächtigen Neubarock-Gliederung und dem markanten Erkerturm.

At the upper end of the main square, between the parish church and the hospital church, architectural accents are set by the quaint turret above the entrance to the former Müllerbräu cellar beer hall, which until the Second World War was a well-known Pfaffenhofen venue for events (large photo left), and the administrative building of the Müllerbräu brewery (1890/91) with its superb neo-Baroque structuring and distinctive oriel tower.

ıs Haus der Begegnung schließt mit seiner im Stil der Neurenaissance gestalteten Fassade das ıuptplatz-Ensemble nach Westen ab. Seit 1976 ein Kulturzentrum mit Ausstellungsräumen, ıeaterbühne und Bücherei wurde das 1878 fertig gestellte Gebäude ursprünglich als Volksschule richtet. Nach Eröffnung einer eigenen Knabenschule (1898) wurden in dem Gebäude bis zum Bau ›s neuen Schulzentrums am Gerolsbach in den 1960er-Jahren nur noch Mädchen unterrichtet. ›rübergehend nutzte auch die Pfaffenhofener Realschule die alte Mädchenschule noch als Ausweich- ıartier, ehe dann im Jahr 1976 der Umbau zum Haus der Begegnung erfolgte.

With its Renaissance-style facade, the "House of Encounter" completes the ensemble of buildings on the west side of the main square. Originally constructed in 1878 as a primary school, the building has been used as a cultural centre with exhibition rooms, theatrical stage and library since 1976. A separate boys' school opened in the city in 1898. From then on, only girls were educated in the building until the 1960s, when the new school centre was built near the Gerolsbach. For a while, the former girls' school was also used as temporary quarters by the city's middle school before its conversion in 1976 into a community centre.

Die Fassaden der stattlichen Bürgerhäuser prägen das Ensemble des Pfaffenhofener Hauptplatzes und schaffen eine beeindruckende Kulisse mit vielen reizvollen Details. Im Bild links die aus dem 19. Jahrhundert stammenden Fassaden des Weilhammer-Anwesens und der ehemaligen Metzgerei Gassner, die bei Neubauten erhalten blieben. Rechts das weitgehend noch im Originalzustand aus der zweiten Hälfte des 19. Jahrhunderts erhaltene Wohn- und Geschäftshaus Hauptplatz 17 mit seiner schönen Wetterfahne.

With their many delightful details, the facades of the handsome town houses are a distinct feature of the ensemble of buildings on Pfaffenhofen's main square and provide an impressive backdrop. The 19th-century facades of the Weilhammer property and the former Gassner butcher's shop (photo left) were preserved when new buildings were constructed. The residential and commercial house with its beautiful weathervane at number 17 on the main square (photo right) has largely preserved its original condition from the second half of the 19th century.

Das alte Café Herb, das in seinen Ursprüngen noch auf die Barockzeit zurückgeht, ist mit seinem Schweifgiebel eines der schönsten historischen Gebäude am oberen Hauptplatz. An den modernen Nachbarn, den Neubau auf dem Bortenschlager-Areal, werden sich die Pfaffenhofener erst noch gewöhnen müssen.
Bild rechts: Blick vom Rathausbalkon auf den Hauptplatz.

In its origins, the old Café Herb dates back to the Baroque period. The curved pediment makes it one of the most beautiful historic buildings at the upper end of the main square. Pfaffenhofen locals will have to get used to its modern neighbour, the new building on the Bortenschlager site.
Photo right: view from the townhall balcony to the main square.

Der Turm der Stadtpfarrkirche und Fahnenstangen spiegeln sich in der Fensterscheibe eines Stadtbusses. Anton Ritzer hat dieses Motiv vor dem Landratsamt eingefangen.
The parish church tower and flagpoles reflected in the window of a municipal bus – a motif captured by Anton Ritzer outside the district administration office.

Zeugen einer großen Pfaffenhofener Brauereitradition sind die stattlichen Gebäude des Kramerbräu und des Salverbräu an der Ecke Auen-/Sonnenstraße. Von den 13 Brauereien, die es im 17. Jahrhundert (bei damals nur 2000 Einwohnern) in Pfaffenhofen gab, sind heute allerdings nur noch zwei übrig geblieben: das Familienunternehmen Müllerbräu und die im Jahr 1922 gegründete Pfaffenhofener Brauhaus AG (Urbanus) als Zusammenschluss der vier alteingesessenen Bierhersteller Wohlherrn, Bortenschlager, Kramer- und Pfaffelbräu.

The handsome Kramerbräu and Salverbräu brewery buildings at the corner of Auenstrasse and Sonnenstrasse bear witness to a great brewing tradition in Pfaffenhofen. However, of the 13 breweries operating in Pfaffenhofen in the 17th century (for only 2,000 inhabitants), only two remain day: the family-owned Müllerbräu, and the joint-stock company Pfaffenhofener Brauhaus AG (Urbanus), founded in 1922 as a merger by four old-established beer producers: Wohlherrn, Bortenschlager, Kramerbräu and Pfaffelbräu.

Zu den Urgesteinen der Pfaffenhofener Brau- und Wirtshaustradition gehören das Hotel Müllerbräu mit seiner prächtigen Stuck verzierten Fassade neben dem Rathaus (Bilder links), der noch aus dem 16. Jahrhundert stammende Stegerbräu in der Ingolstädter Straße (großes Bild unten) sowie das Gasthaus Jungbräu (großes Bild Seite 53 innen) und der Pfaffelbräu (Bilder rechts außen) auf der Südseite des Hauptplatzes.

Among the veterans of Pfaffenhofen's brewing and pub tradition are the Hotel Müllerbräu with its splendid stuccoed facade, located next to the town hall (photos left), the Steger Bräu, dating from the 16th century in Ingolstädter Strasse (bottom right), the Jungbräu (page 53, left) and the Pfaffelbräu (page 53, photos right) on the south side of the main square.

GASTHOF JUNGBRÄU
JUNGBRÄU

Gasthaus Pfaffelbräu

Reste der mittelalterlichen Wehrmauer, die 400 Jahre lang den Stadtkern von Pfaffenhofen umgab, findet man heute noch an der Grabengasse (Bild unten), an der oberen und unteren Stadtmauer sowie am Stadtgraben. Vermutlich kurz nach der Zerstörung des Ortes durch den Stadtbrand von 1388 hatten die Bürger mit dem Bau der Wehranlage begonnen, der um 1438 vollendet war. In diesem Jahr ist Pfaffenhofen auch erstmals urkundlich als Stadt erwähnt. Ab 1807 wurden große Teile der Stadtmauer abgetragen. Das schmale Häuschen an der Ingolstädter Straße 23 (links oben) erinnert noch an die einstige Zollwärter-Behausung am nördlichen Stadttor.

For 400 years, the medieval centre of Pfaffenhofen was enclosed within a circular wall. Remains of the wall can still be seen at the Grabengasse (bottom photo), along the upper and lower city wall, and at the Stadtgraben. Work on the fortification, which presumably began shortly after the fire that destroyed the town in 1388, was completed in 1438. This is also the year in which Pfaffenhofen is first mentioned in a document as a town. Large parts of the city wall began to be torn down from 1807 on. The little house at 23 Ingolstädter Strasse (top left) reminds one of the dwellings that used to accommodate the customs officers at the city's north gate.

Von den ehemals 17 Wehrtürmen sind heute noch zwei erhalten geblieben: einer an der oberen Stadtmauer (siehe Seite 13), und der Pfänderturm, auch Hungerturm genannt, am Stadtgraben (rechts). Hier waren säumige Schuldner aber auch andere Missetäter inhaftiert. Der so genannte Flaschlturm am Platzl (Foto Seite 54 rechts oben) gehörte nicht zur eigentlichen Wehranlage, sondern wurde als Sommerhäuschen von hochgestellten Bediensteten der Wittelsbacher Landesfürsten bewohnt. Einige Jahre beherbergte der Flaschlturm auch ein kleines Museum mit dem Nachlass des Dichters Joseph Maria Lutz.

Two of the city's 17 former fortified towers have been preserved: one along the upper town wall (see page 13), and the Pfänderturm ("distraint tower"), also known as the Hungerturm ("hunger tower"), located on Stadtgraben (right). This is where defaulting debtors and other offenders were imprisoned. The so-called Flaschlturm am Platzl (page 54, top right) was not part of the actual fortifications, but was used instead as a summer cottage by high-ranking servants in the employ of the Wittelsbach rulers. For a number of years, the Flaschlturm also housed a small museum containing the estate of the writer Joseph Maria Lutz.

Das alte Mesnerhaus in der Scheyerer Straße, urkundlich schon im Jahr 1666 erwähnt, beherbergt eine interessante Sammlung zur Geschichte der Stadt und ihres Umlandes. Schwerpunkt des Museums, das seit 1978 in gemeinsamer Trägerschaft von Stadt und Landkreis Pfaffenhofen betrieben wird, sind die Exponate aus dem Bereich der religiösen Volkskunst. Im Frühjahr 2012 musste das Museum wegen anstehender Sanierungsmaßnahmen bis auf weiteres geschlossen werden.

The former sexton's house on Scheyerer Strasse, mentioned in a document as early as 1666, houses an interesting collection relating to the history of the city and its surrounding region. The museum has been run jointly by Pfaffenhofen – the city and the administrative district – since 1978, and focuses on exhibits from the field of religious folk art. In the spring of 2012, the museum was closed until further notice for scheduled renovation work.

Die ehemalige Direktorenvilla der Süddeutschen Wasserwerke AG Nürnberg an der Schulstraße dokumentiert ein wichtiges Kapitel Pfaffenhofener Industriegeschichte. 1898 errichtete die Gesellschaft auf dem angrenzenden Grundstück ihr Elektrizitätswerk, aus dem später die Isar-Amperwerke (heute E.ON Bayern) hervorgingen.

The former directors' villa on Schulstrasse once belonged to the Süddeutsche Wasserwerke AG Nürnberg and represents an important chapter in Pfaffenhofen's industrial history. In 1898, on the adjacent plot of land, the water utility company built its electricity plant, which later became the Isar-Amperwerke (today: E.ON Bayern).

…ı Kern noch aus dem 17. Jahrhundert stammt das ehemalige Schneider-…hätzl-Anwesen an der Ingolstädter Straße.

…ıe former Schneider-Schätzl property on Ingolstädter Strasse (top left) is still es-…ntially a 17th-century building.

Ein traditionsreiches Pfaffenhofener Vorstadt-Anwesen ist das nach einem früheren Besitzer benannte Moserhäusl, das Anfang des 19. Jahrhunderts am Draht errichtet wurde. Von der neuen Eigentümerin wurde es in den letzten Jahren liebevoll restauriert.

The Moserhäusl, named after its former owner and located in a Pfaffenhofen side street, is a piece of property with a rich tradition. It was erected on Draht at the beginning of the 19th century. In recent years it has been lovingly restored by its new owners.

An der Scheyerer Straße gibt es noch einige Vorstadthäuser, die an das alte Pfaffenhofen erinnern (oben). Ein besonderes architektonisches Schmuckstück ist die um 1865 im so genannten Münchener Maximilians-Stil, benannt nach König Maximilian II., errichtete Villa (mittleres Foto)

Das moderne und das alte Pfaffenhofen begegnen sich an der Türltorstraße (unten links) und an der Frauenstraße. Deren Wahrzeichen ist die 1833 errichtete Mariensäule (unten rechts).

There are still a number of suburban houses on Scheyerer Strasse that recall the Pfaffenhofen of bygone days (top). One particular architectural gem is the villa (centre left) built circa 1865 in the "Munich Maximilian" style, named after King Maximilian II.

Old Pfaffenhofen meets the new on Türltorstrasse (bottom left) and Frauenstrasse. The street's landmark, the Marian column (bottom right), was erected in 1833.

Die alten Werkhallen der Maschinenfabrik Stocker an der Münchener Straße (oben) künden heute noch von den Anfangszeiten der Pfaffenhofener Industriegeschichte. Von 1886 bis nach dem 2. Weltkrieg wurden hier mit großem Erfolg Spezialmaschinen für Brauereien, Sägewerke und andere Unternehmen hergestellt und weltweit vertrieben.

Der Moosburger Hof (Bild links), ein modernes Vier-Sterne-Sterne-Hotel, trägt noch den Namen eines Pfaffenhofener Traditions-Gasthauses, das vor dem Neubau auf dem Eckgrundstück an der Einmündung Münchener-/Moosburger Straße stand. Der ehemalige Wirt Josef Rath, ein überzeugter Sozialdemokrat und Gegner des Nazi-Regimes, schrieb mit seinem Haus ein Kapitel politischer Geschichte: Hier fand 1945 die erste Landesversammlung zur Wiedergründung der bayerischen SPD statt.

On Münchener Strasse, the old factory halls of the Stocker engineering works (top) still testify to the early days of Pfaffenhofen's industrial history. From 1886 until after the Second World War, the company was very successful here in manufacturing specialized machinery for breweries, sawmills and other enterprises, and exporting them worldwide.

The Moosburger Hof (photo left), a modern, 4-star hotel, still bears the name of a traditional Pfaffenhofen restaurant that, until it was rebuilt, used to stand on the plot of land where Münchener Strasse and Moosburger Strasse meet. Its former landlord Josef Rath, an ardent social democrat and opponent of the Nazi regime, and his establishment have their place in political history: it was here in 1945 that the first state assembly for the re-establishmant of the Bavarian Social Democratic Party was held.

IDYLLISCHE WINKEL UND IMPRESSIONEN AUS DEM ALTEN PFAFFENHOFEN

Das turmartige Vorstadt-Häuschen an der Quellengasse erinnert noch an die frühere landwirtschaftliche Nutzung als Hopfendarre (großes Foto außen).
Ein Blickfang ist diese alte Haustüre in der „Weilhammer Klamm“ (kleines Foto).

IDYLLIC SETTINGS AND IMPRESSIONS OF OLD PFAFFENHOFEN

The tower-like little suburban house on Quellengasse recalls its earlier agricultural function as an oast house (large photo).
This old front door in the "Weilhammer Klamm" (small photo) is a real eye-catcher.

Bilder von links: Schöll-Anwesen am Stadtgraben, Fenstergitter der ehemaligen Bäckerei Wagenknecht auf der Insel und historischer Schweifgiebel des früheren Bäcker-Buchner-Anwesens in der Frauenstraße.

Photos (from left): the Schöll property on the Stadtgraben, a window grille at the former Wagenknecht bakery on Ilm island, and a historic curved pediment on the former Bäcker-Buchner property on Frauenstrasse.

Hubers Musikkneipe, ehemals Billard-Café Guggenbichler, und Optiker-Fuchs-Anwesen in der „Weilhammer Klamm".
Huber's music pub (formerly the Guggenbichler billiard café) and the Fuchs optician's premises in the "Weilhammer Klamm".

5.2 LEBENSRAUM STADT: JUNG, BUNT UND VOLL ELAN
LIFE IN THE CITY: YOUNG, COLOURFUL AND FULL OF ENERGY

Jung, voller Elan und Lebensfreude präsentiert sich die Stadt Pfaffenhofen ihren Bürgern und Besuchern vor allem an schönen Sommertagen, wenn die Menschen durch die Einkaufsstraßen flanieren, in den Straßencafés die Sonne genießen und die Kinder zwischen den Wasserfontänen des Flachbrunnens vor dem Rathaus herumtollen (Foto Seite 62). In Pfaffenhofen ist jeder gut aufgehoben, der einerseits die Beschaulichkeit einer Kleinstadt schätzt, andererseits aber auch auf urbane Lebensqualität nicht verzichten will. Von allem das Beste – so lässt sich die besondere Attraktivität der Hallertauer Kreisstadt auf einen Nenner bringen. Hier trifft man überall Freunde und Bekannte auf der Straße, wird in Geschäften und Lokalen noch mit dem Namen begrüßt, ist in wenigen Minuten zum Erholen oder zur sportlichen Betätigung draußen in der freien Natur. Genauso schnell aber auch von der Wohnung am Arbeitsplatz, beim Einkaufen, in der Schule oder in den Ämtern.

Young, full of energy and the joy of living is how Pfaffenhofen presents itself to its citizens and visitors to the city – especially on sunny days from spring to autumn, when people stroll through the shopping streets or enjoy the sun as they sit outside in cafés, and children splash about among the jets of water in the shallow well in front of the town hall (photo page 62). Pfaffenhofen is ideal for anyone who values the tranquillity of a small town but doesn't want to do without the urban quality of life. "The best of everything" describes in a nutshell what's so attractive about this district capital in the Hallertau region. You bump into friends and acquaintances everywhere in the street, are still greeted by name in shops, pubs and restaurants, and are only minutes away from relaxing or playing sports out in the open countryside. And that's also how long it takes to get from your home to your place of work, the shops, school and the various municipal authorities.

In eine große Flaniermeile verwandelt sich das Stadtzentrum an den vier verkaufsoffenen Dult-Sonntagen sowie jeden Dienstag und Samstag bei den Wochenmärkten am unteren Hauptplatz.
On the four shopping Sundays in the year when the *Dult* fair is held, and during the weekly markets held at the lower end of the main square every Tuesday and Saturday, the city centre turns into a mile-long boulevard for strollers.

Der grüne Wochenmarkt lockt jeden Dienstag- und Samstagvormittag die Besucher aus dem ganzen Umland auf den Pfaffenhofener Hauptplatz (Bild oben). Heimische Landwirte, Gärtner und Gemüsebauern bieten hier ihre Produkte aus eigenem Anbau an, zum Beispiel frischen Spargel, der im Frühjahr auf den Feldern rund um die Kreisstadt geerntet wird. Dazwischen verkaufen Obst- und Feinkosthändler kulinarische Genüsse aus aller Herren Länder und wer es lieber deftiger mag, gibt sich den verlockenden Düften der Hendlbrater und Imbiss-Stände hin.

Italienische Momente in der Hallertau: An schönen Sommertagen genießen die Pfaffenhofener ihren Cappuccino oder ein Weißbier im Straßencafé (Bild Seite 65) oder lassen auf der Ilm-Insel die Seele baumeln (links unten).

Every Tuesday and Saturday morning, the weekly green market lures visitors from the surrounding region to Pfaffenhofen's main square (top photo). Local farmers, gardeners and vegetable growers offer their home-grown produce for sale, including fresh asparagus harvested locally in spring in the fields around the city. In between, there are fruiterers and delicatessen food suppliers selling culinary delights from all over the world. And those who like their food a little heartier, the mouth-watering scents wafting over from the roast chicken stands and snack stalls will no doubt do the trick.

Italian moments in the Hallertau: on fine summer days, Pfaffenhofen locals enjoy drinking a cappuccino or a weissbier in a street café (see page 65), or getting away from it all on Ilm island (bottom).

GASTHOF JUNGBRÄU

Der große Pfaffenhofener Flohmarkt lockt jeden vierten Sonntag im Monat Tausende von Raritäten-Sammlern aus ganz Bayern auf den Volksfestplatz. Ein weiterer Trödelmarkt findet jeweils am zweiten Sonntag im Monat auf dem Parkplatz des Kaufland-Marktes an der Joseph-Fraunhofer-Straße statt.

Every fourth Sunday of the month, thousands of curiosity collectors from all over Bavaria flock to the big Pfaffenhofen flea market held on the Volksfestplatz. Another flea market takes place every second Sunday of the month in the Kaufland market car park on Joseph Fraunhofer Strasse.

Große Sprünge auf dem Hauptplatz. Bei den vier Dulten, die jedes Jahr auf dem Hauptplatz stattfinden, haben auch die kleinen Besucher ihren Spaß.

High-flyers on the main square: the four *Dult* fairs held on the square every year are fun events for children, too.

·frischung sucht diese süße Badenixe an einem heißen Sommertag im arienbrunnen.

·sweet bathing beauty at the Marian fountain, trying to stay cool on a hot ·mmer day,

Mit einer effektvollen Illumination und festlicher Musik feierten die Pfaffenhofener im Jahr 2008 den Abschluss der Rathaus-Renovierung. Das im neugotischen Stil zwischen 1865 und 1868 gebaute Verwaltungsgebäude steht auf dem Areal des ehemaligen Heilig-Geist-Spitals, das seit dem Mittelalter den Hauptplatz nach Osten abgeschlossen hatte. Die Glocken der einstigen Spitalskirche hängen heute im Rathausturm. Prunkstück des Rathauses ist der bei der Restaurierung im Originalzustand wieder hergestellte Festsaal mit den lebensgroßen Ölgemälden der bayerischen Könige. Außer dem Bürgerbüro und einzelnen Sachgebieten mit stärkerem Publikumsverkehr ist die gesamte Stadtverwaltung in den Neubau am Sigleck umgezogen.

In 2008, Pfaffenhofen celebrated the completion of renovations at the town hall with spectacular illumination and festive music. The administrative building, built in the neo-Gothic style between 1865 and 1868, stands on the site of the former Hospice of the Holy Spirit, which had closed the main square to the east ever since the Middle Ages. The bells of the former hospital now hang in the tower of the town hall, whose showpiece is the banqueting hall, fully restored to its original state during the renovation of the town hall, and which houses life-size oil paintings of the Bavarian kings. Apart from the citizens' bureau and offices dealing with various matters that involve frequent visits from the public, the entire municipal administration has moved into the new building at Sigleck.

Der Hauptplatz wird vor allem in den Sommermonaten immer wieder zur großen Veranstaltungs- und Festarena, wie zum Beispiel bei der Donau-Classic-Oldtimer-Rallye (oben). Unvergessen sind auch die Liveübertragungen und Jubelfeiern bei den Fußball-Weltmeisterschaften 2006 und 2010.

Especially in the summer months, the main square regularly serves as a major arena for public events and festive occasions – such as the *Donau-Classic-Oldtimer-Rallye* (top). Other unforgettable events are the live broadcasts and celebrations during the 2006 and 2010 FIFA World Cups.

5.3 SO FEIERN DIE PFAFFENHOFENER

In Pfaffenhofen pflegt man noch die alten Traditionen. Das gilt für religiöse Bräuche genauso wie für weltliche Veranstaltungen, die ihren festen Platz im jährlichen Terminkalender haben. Dem Sprichwort, dass man die Feste feiern soll, wie sie fallen, folgen die Pfaffenhofener gerne, zum Beispiel wenn sie in der Silvesternacht das neue Jahr mit einem bunten Feuerwerk begrüßen (Foto Seite 70) oder die Sternsinger der Pfarrei St. Johannes Baptist in den Tagen um den 6. Januar als Heilige Drei Könige durch die Stadt ziehen und um Spenden für Not leidende Kinder in Entwicklungsländern bitten (Seite 71).

THIS IS HOW PFAFFENHOFENERS CELEBRATE

In Pfaffenhofen, people still maintain the old traditions. This goes for religious customs and secular occasions, all of which have their permanent place on the year's calendar of events. The city's inhabitants also like to "celebrate festivals as and when they occur", as the saying goes. Such as on New Year's Eve, when they welcome the New Year with colourful fireworks (see page 70), or when carol singers from the parish of St Johannes Baptist dress up as the Three Wise Men and pass through the steets on the days leading up to the 6th of January, asking for donations to help children in need in the developing countries (page 71).

Alle sieben Jahre tanzen seit 1930 (mit Unterbrechung während des 2. Weltkriegs) die Schäffler des MTV Pfaffenhofen auf den Straßen und Plätzen der Stadt und erinnern an einen uralten Brauch, der im 16. Jahrhundert seinen Ursprung in München hatte. Im Fasching 2012, dem 150. Gründungsjahr des größten Pfaffenhofener Sportvereins, begeisterten die Männer mit den roten Kostümen und den strammen Waden die Zuschauer bei 208 Auftritten.

Every seven years since 1930 (except during the Second World War), the MTV Pfaffenhofen coopers have danced on the streets and squares of the city, reminding us of an age-old custom that has its origins in 16th-century Munich. During the annual carnival season of 2012, the 150th anniversary of the founding of Pfaffenhofen's largest sports club, the sturdy-calfed men in red outfits delighted the crowds in a total of 208 performances.

Am Faschingsdienstag steht der Hauptplatz Kopf. Mit einem bunten Maskentreiben und den Auftritten von Prinzenpaaren und Faschingsgarden aus der ganzen Region feiern die Pfaffenhofener alljährlich das Ende der närrischen Saison.

On Shrove Tuesday, the main square stands on its head. Every year on this day, amid the hustle and bustle of colourful masks, carnival princes and princesses and bright-coated dancing girls from the entire region, Pfaffenhofen's inhabitants celebrate the end of the mad season.

Um die Osterzeit ranken sich besonders viele christliche Bräuche, die in Stadt und Landkreis Pfaffenhofen noch intensiv gepflegt werden. Am Palmsonntag, eine Woche vor Ostern, erinnern die katholischen Christen mit Prozessionen und der Segnung von frischen Weidenzweigen (Foto links) an den Einzug Jesu in Jerusalem. Bei der Auferstehungsfeier in den frühen Morgenstunden des Ostersonntags werden in der Pfaffenhofener Stadtpfarrkirche wie in allen anderen katholischen Gotteshäusern die Osterkerze und das Taufwasser gesegnet (Mitte).
Der Maibaum gehört neben dem Turm der Stadtpfarrkirche zu den Wahrzeichen des Hauptplatzes. Während die Pfaffenhofener den weißblauen Stamm mit den von Schülern gestalteten Motivtafeln (kleines Foto oben) nur alle paar Jahre im Stadtzentrum neu aufstellen, wird der alte Brauch in den meisten Ortsteilen jedes Jahr gepflegt. In vielen Dörfern, wie in Förnbach (großes Bild Seite 75), bringen die starken Männer den oftmals über 30 Meter langen Fichtenstamm noch ohne technische Hilfe mit reiner Muskelkraft in die Senkrechte.

Especially around Easter time, there are many Christian customs that are still keenly observed in the city and the Pfaffenhofen administrative district as a whole. On Palm Sunday, a week before Easter, Catholics recall Jesus's entry into Jerusalem by holding a series of processions and blessing fresh willow branches (left photo). During the celebration of the Resurrection early on Easter Sunday in the parish church, as in all other Catholic churches, the paschal candles are lit and the baptismal water is blessed (centre).
Along with the tower of the parish church, the maypole is one of the landmarks on the main square. Although the blue-and-white pole, with its decorative panels created by schoolchildren (right), is put up anew only every few years in the centre of the city, in most villages this old custom is observed every year. In many villages, such as in Förnbach (large photo on page 75), the spruce trunk, often more than 30 metres tall, is still brought into position and raised by strong men using muscle power alone.

LAND ASTHOF GALSTER

Der Brauch der Bittprozessionen in der Zeit um Christi Himmelfahrt ist auch in der Stadt Pfaffenhofen und in den Ortsteilen weit verbreitet. Bei den Flurumgängen betet die ländliche Bevölkerung um himmlischen Schutz für Felder und Fluren, Menschen und Vieh.

The Rogation processions in the period around Ascension Day are also a widespread custom in Pfaffenhofen and surrounding villages. During the village processions, the rural population prays for heavenly protection for their fields and meadows, themselves and their livestock.

Stolz präsentieren die Mitglieder des Trachtenvereins Ilmtaler Pfaffenhofen bei besonderen Anlässen die traditionelle Festtagskleidung der Hallertau. Die Frauen schmücken den Kopf mit einer bestickten Riegelhaube oder filigranen Krönchen. Über dem Kleid aus bunt bedruckter Seide oder feinem Wollstoff trägt die traditionsbewusste Frau ein schwarzes mit silbernen Knöpfen und Ketten besetztes Mieder und eine einfarbige oder auch gemusterte Seidenschürze. Auch das seidene Schultertuch mit Fransen gehört zur Holledauer Tracht.
Typisch für die Tracht der Holledauer Männer sind der flache, breitkrempige Filzhut und die fast bis zum Knie reichenden Stiefel mit den charakteristischen Falten. Damit diese auch zur Geltung kommen, wird die lange Lederhose in die Stiefel gesteckt. Über der mit Silberknöpfen geschmückten Weste, meist aus Samt oder roter Seide, trägt der Holledauer den ebenfalls mit Silberknöpfen besetzten kurzen Janker aus brauner Wolle oder in der kälteren Jahreszeit einen knielangen, eng geschnittenen Bratenrock (Mantel).

On special occasions, members of the Ilmtaler Pfaffenhofen society for traditional costumes are proud to wear the festive clothing of the Hallertau region. The women decorate their hair with an embroidered cap or small, filigree crown. The tradition-conscious among them wear a black bodice decorated with silver buttons and chains on top of their dresses of brightly printed silk or fine wool, plus a plain-coloured or patterned silk apron. The fringed silk shawl is also part of the traditional Holledau costume.
Typical features of the traditional Holledau costume for men are the flat, wide-brimmed felt hat and almost knee-length boots with their characteristic folds. To show the latter off to their best advantage, the long lederhosen are tucked into the boots. A velvet or red-silk waistcoat studded with silver buttons is worn under a short, brown, woollen jacket also decorated with silver buttons. During the winter months, a knee-length, close-fitting frock coat known as a *Bratenrock* is worn instead of the jacket.

Bei der Nacht der Kunst verwandelt sich das Pfaffenhofener Stadtzentrum alljährlich in eine einzige große Bühne. Die Stadt, örtliche Kulturvereine und die Einzelhändler der Interessengemeinschaft Lebendige Innenstadt präsentieren an diesem Abend ein buntes Angebot an Musik, Tanz und Showeinlagen, darunter spektakuläre Akrobatik auf zwei Rädern mit den Vespa-Freunden München im Sommer 2012 (Bild unten). Eingebunden ist die Nacht der Kunst in das Programm des Pfaffenhofener Kultursommers, der fünf Wochen lang mit Konzerten, Ausstellungen, Lesungen und vielen andere Attraktionen Tausende von Besuchern in die Kreisstadt lockt.

Every year, for the Night of Music, the centre of Pfaffenhofen is transformed into a huge stage when the city, its local cultural associations and a retailers' interest group for the promotion of a vibrant inner city present a wide range of music, dance and show interludes, including spectacular acrobatics on two wheels performed in the summer of 2012 by Vespa-Freunde München (Photo bottom). The Night of Music is part of Pfaffenhofen's overall summer programme of cultural events: five weeks of concerts, exhibitions, public readings and many other attractions that draw thousands of visitors to the city.

Seite 79: Bayerische Lebensart und multiku turelle Folklore treffen in Pfaffenhofen imme wieder zusammen, wenn in der Stadt groß Feste gefeiert werde

Photo on page 79: The Bavarian way of life an multicultural folklore frequently come togeth in Pfaffenhofen when major celebrations a held in the streets of the ci

„Ozapft is!", heißt es immer am ersten Freitag im September, wenn in der Kreisstadt das Pfaffenhofener Volksfest beginnt. Mit zünftiger Blasmusik begleitet die Stadtkapelle den offiziellen Wiesnauszug vom Rathaus zum Festplatz. Dort erwartet die Gäste ein großer Vergnügungspark mit vielen Attraktionen und ein buntes Veranstaltungsprogramm in der 5000 Besucher fassenden Festhalle. Zu den Höhepunkten der Pfaffenhofener Wiesn gehören das traditionelle Prunkfeuerwerk und das Steinheben. Mit zwölf Tagen ist das Pfaffenhofener Volksfest nach der Münchener Wiesn eines der längsten in ganz Bayern.
Die Veranstaltung geht auf die Altenstädter Kirchweih zurück, die schon Anfang des 17. Jahrhunderts gefeiert wurde. In seiner heutigen Form gab es das Volksfest zum ersten Mal im Jahr 1929. Nach einer zehnjährigen Zwangspause wegen des 2. Weltkrieges wurde die Pfaffenhofener Wiesn 1949 wieder belebt und findet seither ohne Unterbrechung alljährlich in der ersten Septemberhälfte statt. Bei der Festwoche 2011 konsumierten die Besucher insgesamt 64 500 Maß Bier und 280 Hektoliter alkoholfreie Getränke.

As soon as the cry of *O'zapft is!* goes up in Pfaffenhofen on the first Friday in September, the city's *Volksfest* gets underway. With drums beating and trumpets sounding, the town band accompanies the official parade from the town hall to the fairground, where a huge amusement park with many attractions awaits visitors, along with a diverse programme of events in the festival hall, which can hold 5,000 people. Among the traditional highlights of the Pfaffenhofen beer festival are the spectacular fireworks and the stone-lifting competition. After Munich's *Oktoberfest*, Pfaffenhofen's 12-day *Volksfest* is one of the longest in all of Bavaria.
This event dates back to the *Altenstädter Kirchweih*, an annual parish fair that was held as long ago as the early 17th century. The *Volksfest* as we know it today began in 1929. After a compulsory 10-year break because of the Second World War, the Pfaffenhofen beer festival was revived in 1949 and has been held in the first half of September every year since then. In 2011, visitors consumed a total of 64,500 litres of beer and 28,000 litres of non-alcoholic drinks.

SUPER

Pfaffenhofen: ein Wintermärchen. Anziehungspunkt für Tausende von Besuchern aus der näheren und weiteren Umgebung ist jedes Jahr in der Adventszeit der Christkindlmarkt auf dem Platz vor dem Rathaus. Vier Wochen bieten hier zahlreiche Händler, Glühwein- und Imbissverkäufer in den liebevoll dekorierten Hütten Weihnachtsschmuck, Krippenfiguren, kunstgewerbliche Geschenke und kulinarische Genüsse an. Daneben gibt es ein stimmungsvolles Rahmenprogramm mit einer lebenden Krippe, Weihnachtswichteln und vielen weiteren Attraktionen. Für Gänsehaut-Feeling sorgt immer wieder das Engelsspiel mit Gesang auf dem Rathausbalkon. Vorweihnachtliche Atmosphäre in der gesamten Innenstadt verbreitet auch der Lichtkalender mit einer bunten Illumination zahlreicher Häuserfassaden.

Pfaffenhofen: a winter wonderland. Every year during the Advent season, the Christmas market outside the town hall is a centre of attraction for thousands of visitors from near and far. For four weeks, visitors can buy Christmas decorations, nativity figurines and craftwork, and enjoy a range of culinary delights, available at the lovingly decorated huts and stands of the many traders and vendors of mulled wine and snacks. This is accompanied by a number of festive fringe events, including a live nativity scene and Christmas elves, as well as many other attractions. The angels singing on the balcony of the town hall are an unforgettable experience that's sure to give you goose pimples. The "calendar of lights" – many brightly illuminated house fronts – also provides a pre-Yuletide atmosphere throughout the entire city centre.

Trend-Shop

5.4 KULTURELLES LEBEN
CULTURAL LIFE

Trotz großer Konkurrenz durch die Kulturmetropolen München, Ingolstadt, Augsburg und Regensburg hat es Pfaffenhofen geschafft, ein eigenständiges und vielfältiges Kulturleben auf beachtlichem Niveau zu entwickeln. Für neuen Schwung sorgte vor allem Steffen Kopetzky, künstlerischer Leiter der Biennale 2008 in Bonn und vielfach ausgezeichneter Schriftsteller (neben dem Kulturförderpreis der Stadt Pfaffenhofen erhielt er unter anderem den Preis des Landes Kärnten beim Ingeborg-Bachmann-Wettbewerb). Der in Pfaffenhofen aufgewachsene und lange in Berlin und Hamburg lebende Autor wurde nach der Rückkehr in seine Heimat bei der Kommunalwahl 2008 in den Stadtrat gewählt, wo er das Kulturreferat übernahm. Unter seiner Ägide findet die Pfaffenhofener Kulturszene zunehmend auch überregionale Beachtung, etwa mit einer großen Beuys-Ausstellung oder literarischen Projekten wie einem Island-Festival am Rande der Frankfurter Buchmesse 2011.

Ein prall gefülltes Programm mit Lesungen, Ausstellungen, Theater und Konzerten renommierter Künstler aus dem In- und Ausland präsentiert jedes Jahr der städtische Kultursommer. Die Stadt fördert aber auch ihre eigenen Künstler, indem sie ihnen Konzert-, Theater- und Ausstellungsräume zur Verfügung stellt. In der städtischen Musikschule können Kinder und Jugendliche kostengünstig ein Instrument erlernen. Besondere Talente in allen Sparten der bildenden und darstellenden Kunst würdigt die Stadt alljährlich mit der Verleihung des Kulturförderpreises. Wie urbane Subkultur auch das Leben in der Provinz bereichern kann, beweist das Programm „Be inspired", bei dem junge Graffiti-Sprüher Mauern im öffentlichen Raum für ihr kreatives Hobby nutzen dürfen. Der Jugendmusik-Wettbewerb „Saitensprung" gibt Nachwuchsbands jedes Jahr die Chance, ihr Talent bei einem Open-Air-Konzert vor einem großen Publikum zu beweisen.

Despite tough competition from the cultural metropolises of Munich, Ingolstadt, Augsburg and Regensburg, Pfaffenhofen has managed to develop a rich cultural life of its own with an impressively high standard. Fresh impetus has come primarily from Steffen Kopetzky, artistic director of Biennale 2008 in Bonn and multi-award-winning novelist (in addition to the Cultural Award from the City of Pfaffenhofen, he has also won the prize awarded by the Austrian state of Carinthia at the Ingeborg Bachmann competition). After his return to his home town, the author, who grew up in Pfaffenhofen and later spent long periods in Berlin and Hamburg, was voted into the town council in the 2008 communal elections, where he took over the department of arts and culture. Under his guidance, Pfaffenhofen's cultural scene has earned increasing recognition even on a national level – with the major Joseph Beuys exhibition, for example, and such literary projects as the Island Festival, held on the fringes of the 2011 Frankfurt Book Fair.

The city's annual cultural summer programme includes readings, exhibitions, theatrical performances and concerts by renowned artists from Germany and abroad. The city also promotes its own artists by making concert, theatre and exhibition space available to them. At the municipal music school, children and teenagers can learn to play a musical instrument at little expense. Those with exceptional talent in any branch of the fine arts and performing arts are honoured every year with the city's Cultural Award. The "Be Inspired" programme, in which young graffiti sprayers are permitted to use walls in public spaces for their creative hobby, shows the extent to which an urban subculture can also enrich life in the provinces. The *Saitensprung* music competition for young people gives talented up-and-coming bands an opportunity to perform in front of a large crowd at an annual open-air concert.

Urbane Kunst in der Provinz: Viele Mauern im öffentlichen Raum überlässt die Stadt Pfaffenhofen den jungen Graff
Künstlern für ihr Hobby. Im Bild Sebastian Daschner, einer der Pioniere der örtlichen Sprüher-Sze
Photo on page 85: urban art in the provinces. Pfaffenhofen allows young graffiti artists to indulge in their hobby on ma
of its walls in public spaces. Shown here is Sebastian Daschner, one of the pioneers of the local sprayer sce

Die alte Werkhalle der ehemaligen Zahnradfabrik Herion (Bild oben) dient der Stadt Pfaffenhofen als Kultursaal für Ausstellungen, Lesungen, Konzerte und andere Veranstaltungen. Überregionale Beachtung fand dort im Sommer 2011 eine dreiwöchige Beuys-Ausstellung des Neuen Pfaffenhofener Kunstvereins. Rund 1600 Besucher sahen die Werkschau mit über 200 Exponaten des Künstlers.
Im Bild (Mitte) einer der Initiatoren, Manfred „Mensch" Mayer, mit zwei für die Ausstellung gestalteten Stempeln. Das einer Zeichnung von Beuys nachempfundene Hasen-Motiv konnte sich jeder Besucher im Sinne des Gedankens der „sozialen Skulptur" eigenhändig auf seine Ausstellungszeitung drucken.

Bild unten: Ausstellungseröffnung in der städtischen Galerie im Haus der Begegnung: Der Maler Josef Kroha, Träger des Lovis-Corinth-Preises und einer der überregional renommiertesten Künstler seiner Heimatstadt, im Gespräch mit dem Schriftsteller und städtischen Kulturreferenten Steffen Kopetzky.

The old workshop of the former Herion cog factory (top photo) now serves as a cultural hall for exhibitions, readings, concerts and other events. The three-week Joseph Beuys exhibition held there in the summer of 2011 by the Neuer Pfaffenhofener Kunstverein gained nationwide recognition. About 1,600 people came to see the more than 200 Beuys exhibits on show. One of its initiators, Manfred "Mensch" Mayer (centre), is seen here holding two stamps created for the exhibition. In keeping with the idea of "social sculpture", each visitor was able to stamp his or her own exhibition catalogue with the hare motif, which was based on a drawing by Beuys,

Bottom photo: opening of the exhibition at the "House of Encounter" gallery, with the artist Josef Kroha, holder of the Lovis Corinth Prize and one of Pfaffenhofen's nationally most renowned artists, seen here in conversation with the author Steffen Kopetzky, city councillor in charge of the arts.

Bilder Seite 87: Zu den Höhepunkten im musikalischen Veranstaltungskalender der Stadt Pfaffenhofen gehört das Neujahrskonzert, das der Kammerchor a-capella-nova und das Orchester der Pfarrei St. Johannes Baptist unter der Leitung von Maximilian Penger mit namhaften Solisten alljährlich in der Stadtpfarrkirche präsentieren (links oben).

Hochkarätige Solisten und Ensembles von überregionalem Rang, wie das Gewandhaus Brass Quintett aus Leipzig, gastieren bei den Pfaffenhofener Rathauskonzerten, die seit vielen Jahren während des Winterhalbjahres im historischen Festsaal stattfinden (rechts oben).

Musikalischer Höhepunkt und Abschluss des Pfaffenhofener Kultursommers ist jedes Jahr ein Openair-Konzert auf dem Sparkassenplatz mit bekannten Formationen wie der bayerischen Newcomer-Erfolgsband Django 3000, die 2012 mit ihrem Hit „Heidi" die Fans begeisterte (großes Foto unten).

Photos on page 87: Pfaffenhofen's New Year's concert, per formed by the a-capella-nova chamber choir and St Johan nes Baptist parish church orchestra with eminent soloists and led by Maximilian Penger (top left), is one of the highlights of the city's musical calendar of events.

Top-class soloists and ensembles of national renown, suc as the Gewandhaus Brass Quintett from Leipzig, give gues performances at the Pfaffenhofen town hall concerts, which have been held in the historic banqueting hall durin the winter months for many years (top right).

A musical high point and the closing event of Pfaffenhofen Cultural Summer is the annual open-air concert held on Sparkassenplatz with well-known line-ups, such as the successful newcomer band Django 3000, who delighted their fans in 2012 with their hit "Heidi"
(large photo, bottom).

15.6. - 22.7.
22. JULI 2012

Fast schon Kultstatus hat Wacky Singers Künstlerwerkstatt an der Münchener Straße (Bilder oben). Der Pfaffenhofener Musiker, Schreiner und Holzbildhauer öffnet seit 1996 seine Werkstatt – mittlerweile mit Unterstützung eines engagierten Fördervereins – für Konzerte und Ausstellungen. Wo tagsüber die Hobelmaschinen und Sägen laufen, geben sich abends Newcomer und bekannte Jazzformationen ein Stelldichein. Dass auch internationale Topstars immer wieder den Weg nach Pfaffenhofen finden, liegt an der einzigartigen Atmosphäre, die der Künstlerwerkstatt den Ruf als originellster Jazzclub Bayerns eingebracht hat. Die Stadt Pfaffenhofen ehrte Wacky Singer und seine Künstlerwerkstatt im Jahr 2010 mit dem Kulturförderpreis.
Zu den Trägern dieser Auszeichnung (1994) gehört auch das Kabarett Stachelbär (Bild unten), das seit 1982 die lokale und die überregionale Politik, Prominente und Amtsträger satirisch aufs Korn nimmt. Zum Starkbier-Derblecken der Stachelbären mit den Dellnhauser Musikanten strömen jedes Jahr einige Tausend Besucher nach Pfaffenhofen.

Wacky Singer's artists' workshop on Münchener Strasse (top photos) has virtually achieved cult status. Since 1996, the Pfaffenhofen musician, joiner and wood-carver has made his workshop available for concerts and exhibitions – and is now sponsored in this by a society of dedicated supporters. During the day, the workshop buzzes with the sound of saws and planing machines, but at night, it turns into a meeting place for newcomers and well-known jazz groups. What regularly attracts international stars to Pfaffenhofen is the unique atmosphere at the workshop, which has earned it the reputation of being Bavaria's most original jazz club. In 2010, Pfaffenhofen honoured Wacky Singer and his workshop with the city's Cultural Award.
Previous winners (1994) include the satirical artists Stachelbär (bottom photo), who have been satirizing local and national politicians, celebrities and officials since 1982. Every year, thousands of visitors flock to Pfaffenhofen to watch Stachelbär poke fun during the strong-beer season to the music of the Dellnhauser Musikanten.

Erfolgreiche Künstler aus Pfaffenhofen
Successful Artists from Pfaffenhofen

Professor Gerhard Weinberger, 1948 in Pfaffenhofen geboren, ist einer der profiliertesten Kirchenmusiker Deutschlands. Der 2. Preisträger im Fach Orgel beim ARD-Musikwettbewerb 1971 lehrte an den Musikhochschulen in München, Detmold und Würzburg und veröffentlichte bisher etwa 50 CDs, darunter eine Gesamteinspielung der Orgelwerke Johann Sebastian Bachs, die 2009 mit dem Jahrespreis der deutschen Schallplattenkritik ausgezeichnet wurde. Seit 2004 leitet Weinberger auch das Vokalsolisten-Ensemble der Barockakademie an der Hochschule für Musik in Detmold. Als international gefragter Organist führten ihn seine Konzertreisen durch ganz Europa sowie nach Asien, Nord- und Südamerika.

Professor Gerhard Weinberger, born in Pfaffenhofen in 1948, is one of Germany's highest-profile church musicians. He was awarded 2nd prize for organ music at the 1971 music competition organized by Germany's ARD broadcasting corporation. He has taught at the academies of music in Munich, Detmold and Würzburg, and has so far released about 50 CDs, including a recording of the complete organ works of Johann Sebastian Bach, for which he was awarded the German Record Critics' Prize in 2009. Since 2004, Weinberger has directed the Baroque Academy's vocal soloists' ensemble at the Detmold Academy of Music. As an internationally acclaimed organist, his concert tours take him all over Europe, as well as to Asia and North and South America.

Einer der erfolgreichsten Schriftsteller der Kreisstadt ist Nico Bleutge (Jahrgang 1972), der seine Kindheit und Jugend in Pfaffenhofen verbracht hat. Für seine im Verlag C. H. Beck erschienenen Gedichtbände „klare konturen" (2006) und „fallstreifen" (2008), erntete er höchstes Kritikerlob. Die FAZ bezeichnete ihn als einen der bedeutendsten jungen deutschen Lyriker. Neben dem Kulturförderpreis seiner Heimatstadt (2008) erhielt Bleutge zahlreiche weitere Auszeichnungen, darunter den Wilhelm-Lehmann-Literaturpreis und den Erich-Fried-Preis 2012 sowie ein Stipendium in der Villa Aurora von Lion Feuchtwanger in Kalifornien.

One of the city's most successful writers is Nico Bleutge (born in 1972), who spent his childhood and youth in Pfaffenhofen. His books of poetry *klare konturen* (2006) and *fallstreifen* (2008), published by Verlag C. H. Beck, were highly acclaimed by critics, and the national daily *Frankfurter Allgemeine Zeitung* described him as one of Germany's most important young lyric poets. In addition to winning his home town's Cultural Award in 2008, Bleutge has also received numerous other distinctions, including the Wilhelm Lehmann Literature Prize and the Erich Fried Prize in 2012, and residence scholarship at the Villa Aurora in California, the former home of Lion Feuchtwanger.

Der in Pfaffenhofen aufgewachsene und heute in Neuburg lebende Sänger und Gitarrist C.B. Green, bürgerlich Clemens Benecke, feierte mit Rockpop-Hits wie „Somebody turns on the light" Erfolge in den Radio-Charts. Auch in TV-Serien („Bauer sucht Frau") waren Songs von C.B. Green zu hören. Daneben hatte er zahlreiche Auftritte in TV- und Rundfunksendungen sowie bei Konzerten im In- und Ausland. Fünf CDs bzw. DVDs sowie acht Singles hat C.B. Green bereits veröffentlicht. Mit seiner Schwester betreibt der Sänger eine Kleinkunstbühne in Neuburg und veranstaltet regelmäßig seine eigene Konzertreihe „Songwriters Special" im Wolnzacher Hopfenmuseum. 1999 wurde er mit dem Pfaffenhofener Kulturförderpreis und dem deutschen „PopMusiContest" ausgezeichnet.

The singer and guitarist C.B. Green (born Clemens Benecke) grew up in Pfaffenhofen but now lives in Neuburg. His rock-pop hits, such as "Somebody Turns on the Light", enjoyed success in the radio charts, as well as at concerts in Germany and abroad. His songs were also heard on TV programmes such as *Bauer sucht Frau*. C.B. Green has already released five CDs and DVDs, and eight singles. He and his sister run a cabaret theatre in Neuburg and organize their own concert series known as "Songwriter's Special". In 1999, Benecke was awarded Pfaffenhofen's Cultural Award and won the German "PopMusiContest".

Auch der 1965 in Mailand geborene und in Pfaffenhofen aufgewachsene Roberto Di Gioia ist Kulturförderpreisträger seiner Heimatstadt (2004). Als Keyboarder war Di Gioia 18 Jahre lang Mitglied von Klaus Doldingers „Passport" und ist regelmäßig mit bekannten Künstlern wie Udo Lindenberg, Max Herre und Wigald Boning auf Tour. Auch als Studiomusiker und Produzent hat Di Gioia in der Szene einen exzellenten Namen. In der Liste der Topstars, mit denen der Pfaffenhofener Pianist schon arbeitete, finden sich auch Charlie Watts und Keith Richards von den Rolling Stones. Mit seiner eigenen Band „Marsmobil" hat er mehrere CDs aufgenommen und den offiziellen Song „Munich loves You" für die Fußball-Weltmeisterschaft 2006 produziert, der vor allen WM-Begegnungen in der Allianzarena gespielt wurde.

Another winner of Pfaffenhofen's Cultural Award (2004) is Roberto Di Gioia, who was born in Milan in 1965, but grew up in Pfaffenhofen. As a keyboarder, Di Gioia was a member of Klaus Doldinger's Passport for 18 years and toured regularly with well-known artists, such as Udo Lindenberg, Max Herre and Wigald Boning. Di Gioia has also made an excellent name for himself in music circles as a studio musician and producer. The list of top stars that the pianist has already performed with includes Charlie Watts and Keith Richards from The Rolling Stones. He has recorded several CDs with his own band, Marsmobil, and it was Di Gioia who produced "Munich Loves You", the official song for the 2006 FIFA World Cup that was played before every match at Allianz Arena.

Die bildende Kunst, besonders die Malerei, findet in Pfaffenhofen schon immer einen guten Boden. Viele Gemälde mit Motiven seiner zweiten Heimat, wie dieses Bild vom winterlichen Wochenmarkt (Öl auf Leinwand, 1969), hat der Künstler Eduard Luckhaus hinterlassen. 1910 in Russland geboren und in Polen aufgewachsen, war er nach dem 2. Weltkrieg nach Pfaffenhofen gekommen und hier bis zu seinem Tod im Mai 1975 als Sportlehrer am Gymnasium sowie als freischaffender Maler und Werbegrafiker tätig. Anlässlich seines 100. Geburtstages im Jahr 2010 ehrte die Stadt Eduard Luckhaus mit einer vom Neuen Pfaffenhofener Kunstverein gestalteten großen Retrospektive, die rund 3000 Besucher anlockte.

Michael P. Weingartner (†1986), im Selbstporträt mit Pinsel und typischem Zigarillo (Bild unten links) gestaltete als gelernter Kirchenmaler über 250 Gotteshäuser, aber auch unzählige profane Gebäude im Landkreis Pfaffenhofen sowie in Bayern und Österreich. Auch seine Ölgemälde und Hinterglasbilder mit religiösen Motiven, Stillleben, Hallertauer Landschaften und Stadtansichten sind begehrte Sammlerobjekte.

Der Brunnen in der Seniorenanlage St. Josef am Hofberg (unten rechts) wurde von dem 1946 in Pfaffenhofen geborenen Künstler Herbert Klee gestaltet. Heute lebt der erfolgreiche Maler, Zeichner, Karikaturist und Bildhauer in Holzolling bei Weyarn.

Pfaffenhofen has always proved fertile ground for the fine arts, especially painting. The artist Eduard Luckhaus left behind many paintings of his adopted home, such as this wintry scene of the weekly market (oil on canvas; top). Born in Russia in 1910, Luckhaus grew up in Poland and came to Pfaffenhofen after the Second World War. Until his death in May 1975, he worked as a sports instructor at a grammar school and was also a freelance painter and graphic designer. In 2010, on the 100th anniversary of his birth, Pfaffenhofen honoured Eduard Luckhaus with a retrospective of his work. Organized by the Neue Pfaffenhofener Kunstverein art society, the show attracted some 3,000 visitors.

Michael P. Weingartner (†1986), seen here in a self-portrait with a paintbrush and his typical cigarillo (bottom left), was a trained church painter who worked on more than 250 houses of worship, along with a great many secular buildings in the Pfaffenhofen district as well as in Bavaria and Austria. His oil paintings and reverse glass paintings of religious motifs, still lifes, Hallertau landscapes and townscapes are also coveted collector's items.

The fountain at the St Josef am Hofberg senior citizens' complex (bottom right) was designed by the artist Herbert Klee, who was born in Pfaffenhofen in 1946. The successful painter, illustrator, caricaturist and sculptor now lives in Holzolling, near Weyarn.

Neben Josef Kroha (siehe Seite 86) haben sich auch zahlreiche andere Pfaffenhofener Maler wie Sigi Braun und Norbert Käs (Kulturförderpreisträger 2001) auch außerhalb des Landkreises einen Namen gemacht. Mit seinen abstrakten Gemälden findet vor allem Nikolaus Hipp, Professor für Kunst und Wirtschaftswissenschaften an der Universität in Tiflis/Georgien, iberregionale Beachtung.
Sein Neffe Benedikt Hipp zählt zur jüngeren Garde erfolgreicher Pfaffenhofener Maler. Der Schüler von Sean Scully an der Akademie in München erhielt 2004 den Förderpreis des Bezirks Oberbayern für Nachwuchskünstler und 2005 den Kulturförderpreis seiner Heimatstadt. Unter anderem machte er mit der Beteiligung an Ausstellungen in renommierten Galerien wie der Schirn-Halle in Frankfurt von sich reden.
Auch der Pfaffenhofener Kulturförderpreis 2011 ging mit Sebastian Klein an einen jungen Vertreter der bildenden Kunst. Der gebürtige Schrobenhausener, Student an der Kunsthochschule München, ist seit 2006 freiberuflich als Videokünstler und Grafiker in Pfaffenhofen tätig.
n Pfaffenhofen aufgewachsen ist der Maler Christoph Ruckhäberle, dessen Werke bei der ersten Ausstellung des von ihm mit gegründeten Neuen Pfaffenhofener Kunstvereins im Juni 2008 zu sehen waren. Ruckhäberle war Meisterschüler von Arno Rink an der Hochschule für Grafik und Buchkunst in Leipzig und ist als junger Vertreter der so genannten Neuen Leipziger Schule mit seinen Arbeiten im In- und Ausland erfolgreich.

n addition to Josef Kroha (p. 86), many other Pfaffenhofen painters, such as Sigi Braun and Norbert Käs (winner of the 2001 ultural Award), have also made a name for themselves outside he region. The abstract paintings (top right) of Nikolaus Hipp in articular attract attention in Germany. Hipp is professor of art nd business sciences at Tbilisi University, in Georgia.
is nephew Benedikt Hipp ranks among the younger guard of uccessful Pfaffenhofen painters. The master-class student Sean Scully at the Munich Academy received the Upper Bavaan District's Cultural Award for up-and-coming artists in 04, and his home town's Cultural Award in 2005. He made a ame for himself by, among other things, participating in chibitions at renowned galleries, such as the Schirn Kunstlle in Frankfurt.
affenhofen's Cultural Award for the year 2011 also went to a ung representative of the fine arts: Sebastian Klein. Born Schrobenhausen, he studied at the Munich Academy of Fine ts, and has worked as a freelance video artist and graphic tist in Pfaffenhofen since 2006.
other painter who grew up in Pfaffenhofen is Christoph Ruckberle. His works were on show in June 2008 at the first exhiion organized by the Neue Pfaffenhofener Kunstverein, which founded. He was a master-class student of Arno Rink at the llege of Graphic Art and Book Illustration in Leipzig, and a young representative of the so-called New Leipzig School, ckhäberle's works are successful in Germany and abroad.

Benedikt Hipp: „Gumpengold", 2012, Öl auf Faserplatte

Nikolaus Hipp: Ohne Titel, 2009, Öl auf Leinwand

Christoph Ruckhäberle: Ausstellung des Neuen Pfaffenhofener Kunstvereins, Juni 2008.

Sebastian Klein: „Shine on", 2012, Öl auf Leinwand

Joseph Maria Lutz um das Jahr 1970, porträtiert von dem Pfaffenhofener Maler Viktor Gernhard. Heute ist das Gemälde im Besitz der Stadt und hängt im Treppenhaus der nach dem Dichter benannten Volksschule.
A portrait of Joseph Maria Lutz from circa 1970 by the Pfaffenhofen painter Viktor Gernhard. The painting, now owned by the city, hangs in the stairwell of the school that bears his name.

Der Vater des Brandner Kaspar
The Father of Brandner Kaspar

Einer der bekanntesten Söhne Pfaffenhofens ist der Schriftsteller Joseph Maria Lutz. Am 5. Mai 1893 in der Ilmstadt geboren, hat er in Romanen, Kurzgeschichten, Theaterstücken und Gedichten die bayerische Lebensart und die Schönheit seiner Hallertauer Heimat beschrieben. Den größten überregionalen Erfolg feierte der später in München lebende Dichter mit seinem Theaterstück „Der Brandner Kaspar schaut ins Paradies", das 1934 in Dresden uraufgeführt wurde und auch heute noch auf vielen Bühnen gespielt wird. 1968 wurde J. M. Lutz von seiner Heimatstadt Pfaffenhofen zum Ehrenbürger ernannt, am 30. August 1972 starb er in München.

Das literarische Erbe des Schriftstellers bewahrt auch der Pfaffenhofener Theaterspielkreis, der schon zahlreiche erfolgreiche Stücke des Autors wie „Der Geisterbräu" oder „Birnbaum und Hollerstauden" auf die Bühne gebracht hat. Die von Mitgliedern des Vereins erarbeitete Bühnenfassung des autobiografischen Pfaffenhofen-Romans „Der Zwischenfall" (1979 uraufgeführt) wird zum 120. Geburtstag des Dichters im Jahr 2013 als großes Freilicht-Festspiel am Hauptplatz inszeniert.

One of Pfaffenhofen's best-known sons is the writer Joseph Maria Lutz, who was born in this city on the Ilm on 5 May 1893. In his novels, short stories, plays and poems, he described the Bavarian way of life and the beauty of his native Hallertau region. Lutz, who later moved to Munich, celebrated his greatest national success with his stage play *Der Brandner Kaspar schaut ins Paradies*, which premiered in Dresden in 1934 and which is performed in many theatres even today. Lutz was made an honorary citizen of his home town in 1968. He died in Munich on 30 August 1972.

The writer's literary heritage is also preserved by Pfaffenhofen's amateur theatre group, which has already staged many of the writer's successful pieces, such as *Der Geisterbräu* and *Birnbaum und Hollerstauden*. A stage version of Lutz's autobiographical novel about Pfaffenhofen – *Der Zwischenfall* (first performed in 1979) – put together by members of the group is to be performed in 2013 as an open-air festival play to mark the 120th anniversary of the writer's birth.

Der Theaterspielkreis inszenierte im Jahr 2000 das Singspiel „Birnbaum und Hollerstauden" als Freilichtaufführung im Pausenhof der Joseph-Maria-Lutz-Schule.
In 2000, the Pfaffenhofen amateur theatre group staged an open-air performance of the musical play *Birnbaum und Hollerstauden* with great success – in the playground of the Joseph Maria Lutz School.

400 Jahre Handwerkskunst
400 years of craftsmanship

Eine in Deutschland einmalige Handwerkstradition ist im Café Hipp am Pfaffenhofener Hauptplatz noch lebendig. Seit dem Jahr 1610 wird in dem Anwesen das Handwerk des Wachsziehers und Lebzelters ohne Unterbrechung ausgeübt. In einem liebevoll eingerichteten Museum können Besucher Jahrhunderte alte Holzformen und Arbeitsgeräte zur Herstellung von Kerzen, Votivgaben, Wachsfiguren und Lebzelten sehen. Dokumentiert sind hier auch die Anfänge von Hipp-Babykost. Joseph Hipp, der Großvater des heutigen Besitzers, legte in der Wachszieherei und Lebzelterei am Hauptplatz im Jahr 1899 mit der Herstellung von Zwieback-Mehl als Zusatznahrung für seine eigenen Zwillinge den Grundstein für ein heute international erfolgreiches Unternehmen.

There's a handicraft tradition, unique in Germany, that's still alive on Pfaffenhofen's main square. At the Café Hipp, the candle-maker's and gingerbread-maker's craft has been practised on the premises without interruption since 1610. In a lovingly furnished museum, visitors can see centuries-old wooden moulds and tools that were used to make candles, votive offerings, wax figures and gingerbread.
Also documented here are the beginnings of Hipp baby food. Back in 1899, in the candle-making workshop and gingerbread bakery on the main square, Joseph Hipp, the grandfather of the current owner, decided to produce rusk flour as a supplementary food for his own twins. In doing so, he laid the foundation for what today is a thriving international company.

5.5 SPORT UND FREIZEIT
SPORT AND LEISURE

Wer seine Freizeit aktiv gestalten, Sport treiben oder sich einfach nur erholen und die Seele baumeln lassen will, muss in Pfaffenhofen nicht lange suchen. Über 60 Vereine bieten jede Menge Möglichkeiten, sich sportlich zu betätigen. Dazu stehen in der Stadt und in den Ortsteilen zahlreiche Sportanlagen und Spielplätze zur Verfügung. Und nur wenige Minuten vom Zentrum entfernt finden Sportler und Erholungssuchende in der Umgebung der Stadt viele Wege zum Joggen, Wandern und Radfahren mit herrlichen Ausblicken ins Hallertauer Hügelland.

In Pfaffenhofen, those who wish to make the most of their leisure time, play sports or just relax and get away from it all don't have to look far. There are more than 60 clubs offering endless opportunities to take part in sports, with plenty of sports facilities and courts available in the city and nearby villages. And in the surrounding area, just a few minutes away from the city centre, athletes and people looking for relaxation will find many jogging and hiking trails and cycling routes, with magnificent views of the Hallertau region's hilly landscape.

Sprung vom Fünf-Meter-Turm ins kalte Nass. Das Warmfreibad ist im Sommer die am meisten besuchte Freizeiteinrichtung der Stadt (links).
Ein beliebtes Ziel für Spaziergänger und Radfahrer ist die Vereinsgaststätte des MTV Pfaffenhofen mit ihrem gemütlichen Biergarten (rechts).
Weit reicht der Blick bei einer Rast auf der Radtour rund um die Kreisstadt zwischen dem Weiler Seugen und Förnbach (unten).

Jumping into a pool from a five-metre board. In summer, the heated outdoor pool is the city's most frequented recreational facility (left).
The clubhouse restaurant and ba and the inviting beer garden at Pfaffenhofen's largest sports club, MTV Pfaffenhofen, is a popular destination for cyclists and walkers (top right).
There's a clear, unobstructed view for anyone who rests between Förnbach and the tiny village of Seugen while on a cycling tour around the district capital (bottom).

Bilder Seite 95: Die grüne Lunge der Stadt und Erholungsraum für Spaziergäng und Jogger sind die Wälder, die Pfaffenhofen in allen Himmelsrichtungen umg ben. Auch Schwammerlsucher machen hier im Herbst reiche Beu

The forests that surround Pfaffenhofen on all sides are the city's green lung and a r creational space for joggers and walkers. In autumn, they're also a great place mushroom picke

Pfaffenhofen ist ein Mekka für Skater und andere Funsportler. Im Untergeschoss der Kulturhalle auf dem ehemaligen Herion-Werksgelände hat die Stadt für ihre Jugend den größten Indoor-Funpark Bayerns eingerichtet.

Pfaffenhofen is a mecca for those who like skateboarding and other fun sports. For their benefit, the city has set up Bavaria's largest indoor fun-sports arena in the basement of the cultural centre, on the grounds of the former Herion factory.

Der Waldspielplatz des MTV Pfaffenhofen auf der Jahnhöhe bei Reisgang bietet Freizeitsportlern im Sommer ideale Trainingsmöglichkeiten (links).

Direkt beim Pfaffenhofener Schwimmbad sind zwei Trendsportarten zu Hause: Neben der modernen Beachvolleyball-Anlage trotzen die Sportkletterer im PAFRock-Zentrum des Alpenvereins den Gesetzen der Schwerkraft (Fotos rechts und Mitte).

The forest playground at the MTV Pfaffenhofen sports club on the Jahnhöhe, near Reisgang, offers amateur sports enthusiasts ideal training opportunities in summer.

Two trend sports have established themselves right next to Pfaffenhofen's swimming pool: while the beach volleyball enthusiasts practise on their modern facility, the sports climbers at the Alpine Association's PAFRock Centre defy the laws of gravity (right and centre).

Auf der 400 Meter langen Sandbahn des städtischen Stadions liefern sich seit 1949 Speedwayfahrer aus dem In- und Ausland packende Rennen. Mit der Neugestaltung des Areals im Zuge der kleinen Landesgartenschau „Natur in Pfaffenhofen 2017“ werden die Motorsportler an einen anderen Standort umziehen müssen.

Speedway riders from Germany and abroad have been competing in thrilling races on the 400-metre dirt track at the city stadium since 1949. Since the area is going to be re-developed as part of the preparations for the small state garden show "Nature in Pfaffenhofen 2017", the riders will have to move to a new location.

as städtische Sportstadion an der Ingolstädter Straße ist seit den 1930er Jahren Zentrum der Pfaf-
nhofener Fußballer (oben links). In der vom DFB geförderten Kleinfeld-Arena beim Schwimmbad
nnen junge Fußball-Talente dem runden Leder nachjagen (oben rechts).
ssportfreunde treffen sich im Winter auf den zugefrorenen Weihern oder im Kunsteisstadion an der
golstädter Straße. Die Eishockeymannschaft des EC Pfaffenhofen, Schlittschuhläufer und Stock-
hützen finden in der Halle beste Wettkampf- und Trainingsmöglichkeiten (unten).

The city stadium on Ingolstädter Strasse (top left) has been the footballing centre of Pfaffenhofen since the 1930s. Talented young footballers can enjoy a good kickabout at the small-pitch arena (next to the swimming pool), which is sponsored by the German Football Association (top right).
In winter, ice sports enthusiasts meet at the frozen pond or at the ice stadium on Ingolstädter Strasse. The stadium offers ideal training possibilities and opportunities for competitive events for the ice-hockey team of the EC Pfaffenhofen sports club, ice-skaters and curling players (bottom).

5.6

ÖKOLOGISCH UND NACHHALTIG
ECOLOGICAL AND SUSTAINABLE

In Sachen Ökologie und Nachhaltigkeit gehört Pfaffenhofen schon seit Jahren zu den Musterkommunen. Mit der Errichtung eines Biomasse-Heizkraftwerkes (Bild links) im Jahr 2001 erfüllte Pfaffenhofen als erste deutsche Stadt die Vorgaben des Kyoto-Protokolls zum Klimaschutz. Die aus nachwachsenden Hölzern erzeugte Energie versorgt zahlreiche große Betriebe, öffentliche Einrichtungen und Privathaushalte mit Fernwärme, Strom, Kälte und Dampf. Damit können pro Jahr rund 55 000 t Kohlendioxid eingespart werden.

Ein grünes Vorzeigeprojekt ist das Eco-Quartier in Weihern (Grafik rechts unten). Im Umfeld des Biobauernhofes der Familie Hirschberger entstehen ein Siedlungsgebiet und ein Kompetenzzentrum für ökologisch orientierte Unternehmen. Von der Auswahl des Baumaterials bis zur kompletten Energieversorgung aus regenerativen Quellen ist das gesamte Siedlungskonzept am Grundsatz der Nachhaltigkeit ausgerichtet. Auch soziale Einrichtungen für Altenpflege, Kinderbetreuung und Bildung sowie andere Gemeinschaftsprojekte (zum Beispiel Car-Sharing) sind geplant.

Pfaffenhofen has long been a model community when it comes to ecology and sustainability.

With the construction in 2001 of a biomass-fuelled combined heat and power plant (photo left), Pfaffenhofen became the first German city to comply with the Kyoto Protocol on climate change. The energy generated from renewable woods provides many large enterprises, public buildings and private homes with district heating, electricity, refrigeration and steam – reducing carbon dioxide emissions by about 55,000 tons a year.

The Ecoquartier in the Weihern district of the city is a green showcase project (graphic bottom right). Here, a settlement area and a centre of competence are being built near the organic farm belonging to the Hirschberger family. From the choice of building materials to the complete range of energy services from renewable sources, the entire housing concept is based on the principle of sustainability. Also planned are facilities that will provide nursing care for the elderly, childcare and education, along with other joint projects, such as car-sharing.

Starthilfe für den Umstieg in eine umweltfreundliche Mobilität: Auf dem Hauptplatz gibt es eine kostenlose Tankstelle für Elektrofahrzeuge (links).
Die Energiewende ist nicht mehr fern: Hinter dem Turm der Stadtpfarrkirche sieht man von den Hügeln im Wohngebiet an der Sudetenstraße das erste im Landkreis Pfaffenhofen errichtete Windrad bei Frickendorf (rechts).

Jump start for the changeover to an environmentally friendly form of mobility: electric vehicles can recharge for free at this filling station on the main square (left).
The change in energy policy is not far off. The first wind turbine in the Pfaffenhofen administrative district – near Frickendorf – is visible behind the parish church tower, seen here from the hills in the residential area in Sudetenstrasse (right).

Der Naturschutz hat in Pfaffenhofen seit Jahrzehnten einen hohen Stellenwert. Ein Beispiel ist die schon vor einigen Jahren begonnene Renaturierung der Ilm, des Gerolsbaches und weiterer kleinerer Gewässer in der Umgebung der Stadt. Auch der Biber ist hier wieder heimisch geworden. Am so genannten Biberweg zwischen Pfaffenhofen und Förnbach erfahren Spaziergänger auf Infotafeln Wissenswertes über den Lebensraum des possierlichen Nagers (Bild links).
Seit dem Jahr 2004 brüten wieder Störche auf dem vom Bund Naturschutz errichteten Nistplatz über dem Schyren-Gymnasium. Auf den Wiesen am Stadtrand kann man Familie Adebar bei der Futtersuche beobachten (rechts).

Conservation has been rated high in Pfaffenhofen for decades. A good example is the renaturation that began several years ago of the River Ilm, the Gerolsbach and other smaller bodies of water in the area surrounding the city. Beavers are one of the species that have resettled in the area. Along the so-called beaver path between Pfaffenhofen and Förnbach, information panels provide walkers with interesting facts about the habitat of this cute rodent (photo left).
Since 2004, storks have been brooding on nesting sites erected above the Schyren grammar school by the nature conservation association. In the meadows at the edge of the city, the storks can be observed foraging for food (right).

Bilder Seite 103: So nah, so vertraut – und doch so abweisend: Durch ein Korsett aus Betonmauern und steilen Uferböschungen zwängt sich die Ilm auf ihrem Weg durch Pfaffenhofen. Der Fluss den die Stadt in ihrem Namen führt, ist für die Bürger nur an ganz wenigen Stellen zugänglich. Dies soll sich mit den Planungen für die regionale Gartenschau ändern, die im Jahr 2017 unter dem Titel „Natur in Pfaffenhofen an der Ilm" ausgerichtet wird. Bei einem von der Stadt ausgeschriebenen Wettbewerb legten 41 Landschaftsplaner ihre Konzepte vor, um den Fluss wieder näher an die Menschen heranzubringen und die Uferbereiche als Erlebnisraum zu öffnen.
Im Bild unten links der Siegerentwurf des Planungsbüros hutterreimann, Berlin, zur Gestaltung der Ilminsel.
Rechts: Das alte Wehr am ehemaligen Schlachthofgelände, wo ein Bürgerpark entstehen soll.

So close, so familiar, yet still so unapproachable: corseted by concrete walls and steep embankments, the River Ilm pushes its way through Pfaffenhofen. The river that Pfaffenhofen includes in its name can be accessed by locals in only a few places. That will change by the time the regional garden show "Natur in Pfaffenhofen an der Ilm" opens in 2017. In a competition organized by the city, 41 town and country planners presented their concepts on how to bring the river closer to the city's inhabitants again and make the riverbanks accessible as an adventure sphere.
Bottom left: the winning entry, from the hutterreimann planning office in Berlin, for the future design of the Ilm island.
Right: the old weir, next to the premises of the former slaughterhouse. Plans call for a public park to be created here.

B.B's Frisuren

5.7 OPTIMALE INFRASTRUKTUR
OPTIMAL INFRASTRUCTURE

Als lebendiges Mittelzentrum und Verwaltungshauptstadt des Landkreises verfügt Pfaffenhofen über eine perfekte Infrastruktur. Dazu gehören ein funktionierender Nahverkehr mit Bahnanschluss und Stadtbuslinien, ein breit gefächertes Bildungsangebot, zwei Kliniken für die medizinische Grundversorgung und psychisch Kranke, aber auch moderne soziale Einrichtungen von der Kinderkrippe bis zur Seniorenbetreuung. Pfaffenhofen ist auch Sitz vieler Ämter und Behörden. Und nicht zuletzt ist Pfaffenhofen eine lebendige Einkaufsstadt mit über 300 Einzelhändlern, Dienstleistern und Gastronomiebetrieben in der Innenstadt.

As a vibrant regional centre and administrative capital of the Pfaffenhofen district, the city has an ideal infrastructure. This includes a well-functioning public transport system with a railway connection and city bus lines, a wide range of educational possibilities, two clinics providing primary medical care and treatment for the mentally ill, as well as modern social institutions, all the way from nurseries to care for the elderly. Pfaffenhofen is also the seat of many administrative bodies and public authorities. And, not least, it's a lively shopping city with more than 300 inner-city retail traders, service providers and restaurants.

Vom Bahnhof Pfaffenhofen ist ma mit dem Regionalexpress in weniger als einer halben Stunde in München (Bild oben).
Acht Stadtbuslinien verbinden die am Stadtrand gelegenen Siedlungsgebiete mit dem Ortszentrum, den Gewerbegebieten und dem Bahnhof.

The regional express train will get you from Pfaffenhofen to Munich i less than 30 minutes (Photo top).
Eight city bus lines connect the settlement areas on the outskirts town with the city centre, the business parks and the railway station

e im Jahr 1984 eröffnete Ilmtalklinik im Süden der Kreis-
adt ist Zentrum der medizinischen Grundversorgung für den
ndkreis Pfaffenhofen (Foto rechts unten).
n die Behandlung von psychisch kranken Menschen küm-
ert sich die Danuvius-Klinik, die im Jahr 2010 in der Nach-
rschaft der Ilmtalklinik errichtet wurde (links oben).
dem 1912 errichteten Gebäude des staatlichen Vermes-
ngsamtes an der Kellerstraße war früher das Finanzamt un-
rgebracht (oben rechts). Die Steuerbehörde ist mittlerweile
einen Neubau an der Schirmbeckstraße umgezogen (Mitte).

e Ilmtal clinic in the south of the city opened in 1984 and is
primary health care centre for the Pfaffenhofen region
hoto bottom right).
e Danuvius clinic is responsible for treating people with
ental illnesses. It was built in 2010 in the vicinity of the Ilm-
clinic (top left).
e striking-looking building on Kellerstrasse that now hou-
s the state land surveying office (top right) was built
1912. It was previously used by the Pfaffenhofen tax
thorities, who now have their offices in a new building on
hirmbeckstrasse (centre).

Die Joseph-Maria-Lutz-Schule (oben Mitte) ist das älteste Pfaffenhofener Schulgebäude, das heute noch seinem ursprünglichen Zweck dient. 1897 als reine Knabenschule errichtet, werden hier seit dem Jahr 1971 Buben und Mädchen der 1. bis 4. Jahrgangsstufe unterrichtet.
Die Dreifach-Turnhalle der Niederscheyerer Volksschule dient auch als großer Veranstaltungssaal für Konzerte und andere Events (Foto unten).
Über 700 Kindergarten- und Krippenplätze stehen jungen Familien in Pfaffenhofen zur Verfügung, wie hier im Kindergarten Burzlbaam, der als erstes städtisches Passiv-Haus nach ökologischen Konzepten gebaut wurde (oben links).
Im Alten- und Pflegeheim St. Franziskus, 1862 als städtisches Krankenhaus errichtet, werden seit 1984 rund 120 ältere Menschen betreut (oben rechts).

The Joseph Maria Lutz school (top centre) is the oldest school building in Pfaffenhofen that still serves its original purpose. Built in 1897 as a boys-only school, it has been teaching boys and girls (aged between 6 and 10) together since 1971.
The multi-purpose gym at the Niederscheyerer school is also used as a large function hall for concerts and other events (bottom).
In Pfaffenhofen, there are more than 700 kindergarten and day-nursery places available to young families, such as the Burzlbaam kindergarten (top left), the first municipal passive house to be built according to ecological concepts.
The St Franziskus residential and nursing care complex for the elderly (top right) was originally built in 1862 as a municipal hospital. It has been looking after about 120 senior citizens since 1984.

Ein Bild des Kirchenmalers Michael P. Weingartner ziert die Fassade der im Jahr 1951 gebaute Landwirtschaftsschule und Fachschule für Hopfenbau in Pfaffenhofen (großes Foto rechts). Sie trägt heute den Namen ihres ehemaligen Leiters Dr. Hans Eisenmann († 1987). Der spätere Pfaffenhofener Landrat und bayerische Landwirtschaftsminister ist Ehrenbürger seiner Heimatstadt Pfaffenhofen.

Über 2600 Jugendliche aus dem ganzen Landkreis besuchen das Pfaffenhofener Schyren-Gymnasium (oben links) und die Georg-Hipp-Realschule (unten links).

The image that graces the facade of Pfaffenhofen's agricultural college and technical college for hop-cultivation (built in 1951) was created by the church painter Michael P. Weingartner (right). The building today bears the name of its former director, Dr. Hans Eisenmann (†1987). Eisenmann later became a district administrator and served as a Bavarian minister of agriculture, and was made an honorary citizen of Pfaffenhofen, his home town.

More than 2,600 youngsters from all over the administrative district attend Pfaffenhofen's Schyren grammar school (top left) and the Georg Hipp secondary modern school (bottom left).

5.8 GUTER BODEN FUR DIE WIRTSCHAFT
FERTILE GROUND FOR THE ECONOMY

Pfaffenhofen ist ein guter Boden für Industrie, Handel, Handwerk und Dienstleister. Neben vielen mittelständischen Traditionsunternehmen wie den beiden Brauereien Müllerbräu und Urbanus (Fotos unten) sind in der Kreisstadt auch international tätige Firmen ansässig, zum Beispiel der Kleiderbügel-Hersteller MAWA (links oben). Der Stromerzeuger E.ON Bayern ist mit seinem Kundencenter, einem Ausbildungszentrum und Lehrwerkstätten für 150 Azubis auf dem Gelände der ehemaligen Isar-Amperwerke am Draht ansässig (oben rechts).

Pfaffenhofen is an ideal location for industry, trade, craftsmen and service providers. Aside from the many traditional medium-sized companies, such as the Müllerbräu and Urbanus breweries (bottom photos), Pfaffenhofen is also home to a number of international firms, for example the coat-hanger manufacturer MAWA (top left). The electricity producer E.ON has located its customer centre, training centre and apprentice workshops for 150 trainees on the grounds of the Isar-Amperwerke on Draht (top right).

Die Vereinigten Sparkassen des Landkreises sind neben mehreren anderen Banken in der Kreisstadt mit ihrer modernen Zentrale und Zweigstellen vertreten (Bild unten).
Auch der japanische Elektronik-Konzern Panasonic ist nach einem Joint Venture mit der 1974 gegründeten Firma MS-Relais in Pfaffenhofen ansässig. Ein Produktionsstandort und das europäische Zentrallager befinden sich im Ortsteil Weihern (oben links).
Im Gewerbegebiet Kuglhof haben sich in den letzten Jahren zahlreiche Firmen aus unterschiedlichen Branchen, darunter ein Multiplex-Kino (oben rechts), mehrere Gastronomiebetriebe, ein Bowlingcenter, Autohändler, Ingenieurbüros und viele weitere Betriebe angesiedelt.

Among the various banks represented in Pfaffenhofen are the district's united savings banks with their modern corporate and branch offices (bottom). Since its joint venture with the MS-Relais company (founded in 1974), the Japanese electronics group Panasonic has based its production location and main European distribution centre in the Weihern part of Pfaffenhofen (top left).
In recent years, numerous companies from various market segments have settled in the Kuglhof commercial area – including a multiplex cinema (top right), several restaurants, a bowling centre, car dealership, engineering offices and many other businesses.

BIO-QUALITÄT AUS ÜBERZEUGUNG
ORGANIC QUALITY OUT OF CONVICTION

Das wichtigste und bekannteste Unternehmen der Kreisstadt ist der Babynahrungshersteller Hipp, weltweit größter Verarbeiter von Produkten aus biologischer Landwirtschaft. Seine Wurzeln hat das Unternehmen am Pfaffenhofener Hauptplatz, wo der Konditormeister Joseph Hipp 1899 erstmals Zwiebackmehl als Ergänzungsnahrung für die eigenen Kinder herstellte. Dessen Sohn Georg lagerte 1932 den schnell wachsenden Betriebszweig in eine ehemalige Hopfenhalle an der Münchener Straße aus und legte nach dem 2. Weltkrieg mit der Herstellung von Obst- und Gemüsebrei den Grundstein zur industriellen Großproduktion von Babynahrung.

Nach dem frühen Tod des Firmengründers im Jahr 1967 übernahm dessen Sohn Claus, damals 29 Jahre alt, das Unternehmen, das er heute noch mit seinem Bruder Paulus und seinen Söhnen Sebastian und Stefan führt. Den Weg des Bio-Pioniers Georg Hipp, nur Rohstoffe zu verwenden, die aus biologischem Anbau ohne Einsatz von chemischen Dünge- und Pflanzenschutzmitteln stammen, setzen seine Nachfolger bis heute konsequent fort. Claus Hipps persönliches Versprechen, „Dafür stehe ich mit meinem Namen", ist für das Pfaffenhofener Familienunternehmen nach wie vor ein bedeutender Wettbewerbsvorteil gegen die Konkurrenz der großen internationalen Lebensmittelkonzerne. Der Jahresumsatz des Hippwerkes, dessen Bio-Produkte nicht nur Babys, sondern auch Sportler und Senioren schätzen, belief sich im Jahr 2011 auf rund 550 Millionen Euro. In sieben europäischen Ländern – von der Schweiz bis Russland – beschäftigt Hipp rund 2000 Mitarbeiter, davon 1000 am Stammsitz in Pfaffenhofen.

The most important and best-known company in the district capital is the baby food manufacturer Hipp, the world's largest processor of organically farmed produce. The company's roots date back to 1899 and the main square in Pfaffenhofen, where the master confectioner Joseph Hipp first produced rusk flour as a supplementary food for his own children. In 1932, his son George transferred this rapidly growing branch of the business to Münchener Strasse, to a hall once used by the hop-growing industry. After the Second World War, with the production of fruit and vegetable purée, he laid the foundation for the industrial large-scale production of baby food.

After the early death of the company founder in 1967, the company was taken over by his 29-year-old son Claus, who runs it today with his brother Paulus and his sons Sebastian and Stefan. The path chosen by Georg Hipp, a pioneer in organic production – to use only raw materials that have been organically farmed without the use of chemical fertilizers and pesticides – is still being consistently followed by his successors. Claus Hipp's personal promise of staking his reputation on his products remains the Pfaffenhofen company's key competitive advantage over the major international food giants. Annual turnover at Hipp, whose bio products are loved not only by babies, but also by sportsmen and the elderly, totalled about 550 million euros in 2011. Hipp employs around 2,000 people in seven European countries – from Switzerland to Russia – 1,000 of them at the company headquarters in Pfaffenhofen.

Stammhaus von Hipp-Babykost ist die Konditorei und Wachszieherei am Pfaffenhofener Hauptplatz. Hier stellte Joseph Hipp 1899 das erste Zwiebackmehl her.

The original home of Hipp baby food is the confectionery and candle-making workshop on Pfaffenhofen's main square. This is where, in 1899, Joseph Hipp first produced his rusk flour.

Georg Hipp lagerte die Herstellung der Babynahrung 1932 aus dem Konditoreibetrieb der Eltern in eine alte Hopfenhalle aus und legte den Grundstein zur industriellen Großproduktion.

In 1932, Georg Hipp transferred the manufacture of baby food from his parents' confectionery business to a hall once used by the hop-growing industry, thus paving the way for large-scale industrial production.

Firmenchef Professor Dr. Claus Hipp ist seit 2003 Ehrenbürger seiner Heimatstadt Pfaffenhofen. Für sein unternehmerisches Lebenswerk wurde er mit zahlreichen weiteren Ehrungen bedacht, darunter die bayerische Verfassungsmedaille, und die Auszeichnung als „Entrepreneur des Jahres 2010" der Unternehmensberatung „Ernst & Young". Die auf Nachhaltigkeit und ethische Grundsätze ausgerichtete Firmenphilosophie des Unternehmens wurde unter anderem mit der Verleihung des deutschen Solarpreises 2011 und des deutschen Nachhaltigkeitspreises 2009 gewürdigt.

The company boss, Professor Dr. Claus Hipp, was made an honorary citizen of his home city of Pfaffenhofen in 2003. He has received numerous other distinctions for his entrepreneurial life's work, including the Medal of the Bavarian Constitution, and was named Entrepreneur of the Year 2010 by the consulting firm Ernst & Young. Among the honours awarded to Hipp for its company philosophy, based on sustainability and ethical principles, are the German Solar Prize (2011) and Germany's Sustainability Prize (2009).

INNOVATIVE ARZNEIEN AUS PFAFFENHOFEN
INNOVATIVE MEDICINES FROM PFAFFENHOFEN

Ein Unternehmen von Weltrang ist der Pharmakonzern Daiichi Sankyo, der an seinem wichtigsten europäischen Produktionsstandort Pfaffenhofen 450 Mitarbeiter beschäftigt und damit der zweitgrößte Arbeitgeber der Kreisstadt ist. In seinen hochmodernen Produktionsanlagen stellt das Unternehmen jährlich zirka drei Milliarden Tabletten her und exportiert diese in mehr als 50 Länder. Weltweit zählt das börsennotierte Unternehmen, das 2005 aus der Fusion der beiden japanischen Pharma-Konzerne Daiichi und Sankyo hervorgegangen ist, zu den 20 größten der Branche. Rund 32 000 Mitarbeiter sind heute für das Unternehmen tätig.

Im Geschäftsjahr 2011 belief sich der Nettoumsatz auf 8,6 Milliarden Euro, davon entfielen 618 Millionen Euro auf Europa. Der umsatzstärkste Wirkstoff von Daiichi Sankyo ist mit 2,3 Milliarden Euro der Blutdrucksenker Olmesartan. Die gesamte Produktfamilie der Medikamente mit diesem Wirkstoff wird im Werk Pfaffenhofen hergestellt.

Auch in der globalen Produktentwicklung des Konzerns spielt der Standort Pfaffenhofen eine Schlüsselrolle. Beispielsweise erarbeiten die rund 70 Mitarbeiter der Entwicklungsabteilung die optimalen Rezepturen für neue Medikamente des Konzerns. Außerdem werden in Pfaffenhofen unterschiedliche Produktionsmethoden erprobt und die Stabilität neuer Medikamente untersucht.

Die Ursprünge der Arzneimittelproduktion in Pfaffenhofen gehen auf das Luitpoldwerk zurück, das 1910 in München gegründet worden war. Während des Zweiten Weltkrieges verlagerte das Luitpoldwerk die Produktion nach Pfaffenhofen in die Baracken des Reichsarbeitsdienstes am Gerolsbach. 1964 bezog das Unternehmen einen Neubau an der Ingolstädter Straße. 1990 übernahm der japanische Sankyo-Konzern die Firma.

Daiichi Sankyo hat seitdem kontinuierlich in die Erweiterung des Standortes investiert und die Mitarbeiterzahl gesteigert. 2007 weihte der Konzern neue Gebäude für die Tablettenproduktion und Verpackung ein. 2011 wurde ein neues Hochregallager errichtet. Derzeit baut Daiichi Sankyo ein neues Gebäude für die pharmazeutische Entwicklung. Parallel dazu wird die Produktionskapazität schrittweise auf bis zu vier Milliarden Tabletten erhöht.

Das Münchner Stammhaus um 1930.
The Munich headquarters around 1930.

Der 1964 bezogene Neubau in Pfaffenhofen.
The new building the company moved into in 1964.

Seit der Übernahme des ehemaligen Luitpold-Werkes hat der Daiichi-Sankyo-Konzern den Produktionsstandort Pfaffenhofen kontinuierlich ausgebaut.
Since taking over the former Luitpold Werk, the Daiichi Sankyo corporation has continued to expand its Pfaffenhofen production location.

The world-famous Daiichi Sankyo pharmaceuticals company employs 450 people in Pfaffenhofen, its most important European production location, making the Japanese group the second-largest employer in this district capital. At its state-of-the-art production facilities, Daiichi Sankyo manufactures some three billion tablets a year and exports them to more than 50 countries. This publicly traded company – the result of a 2005 merger between two leading Japanese pharmaceutical companies, Daiichi und Sankyo – ranks among the 20 largest in the industry and today employs about 32,000 people worldwide.

In the financial year 2011, net sales amounted to 8.6 billion euros, of which Europe accounted for 618 million euros. Daiichi Sankyo's top-selling active substance is the antihypertensive Olmesartan (2.3 billion euros). The entire product range of medication containing this substance is manufactured at the Pfaffenhofen plant.

As a production location, Pfaffenhofen plays a key role in Daiichi Sankyo's global product development, too. By way of an example, the 70 or so members of staff employed in the development department look for optimal formulas for new drugs. The Pfaffenhofen plant also tests different production methods and analyses new drugs for their stability.

The origins of the drug manufacturing in Pfaffenhofen go back to the Luitpold Werk pharmaceutical company, founded in Munich in 1910. During the Second World War, the Luitpold Werk relocated production to Pfaffenhofen, to the Gerolsbach barracks of the Reich Labour Service. In 1964, the company moved into a new building on Ingolstädter Strasse. It was taken over by Japan's Sankyo corporation in 1990, and since then, Daiichi Sankyo has continued to invest in the expansion of the location and increase the number of employees there. In 2007, the corporation inaugurated new buildings for the manufacture of tablets and for packaging, and erected a new high-rack warehouse in 2011. At present, Daiichi Sankyo is constructing a new building for pharmaceutical development, while at the same time gradually raising its annual production capacity to four billion tablets.

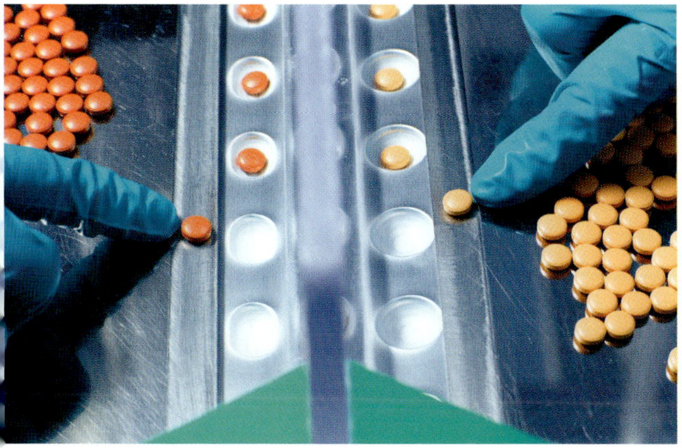

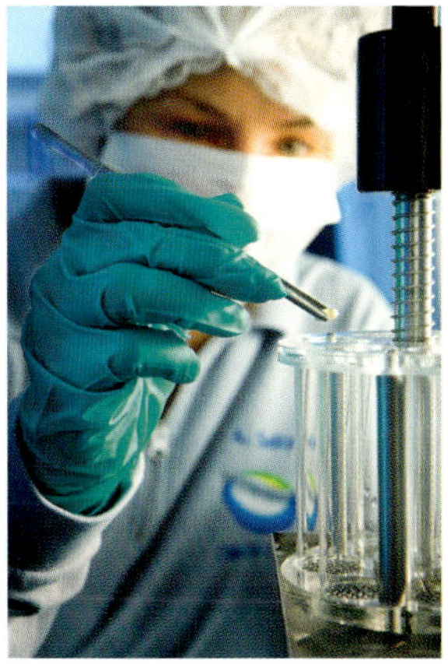

Etwa drei Milliarden Tabletten werden jährlich bei Daiichi-Sankyo in hochmodernen Produktionsanlagen am Standort Pfaffenhofen hergestellt. Auch in der Produktentwicklung des Pharmakonzerns spielt Pfaffenhofen eine Schlüsselrolle.

Some three billion tablets are manufactured at Daiichi Sankyo's ultra-modern production facilities in Pfaffenhofen every year. Pfaffenhofen also plays a key role in the pharmaceutical company's product development.

HEIMAT DES GRÜNEN GOLDES
HOME OF THE GREEN GOLD

Andrehen der jungen Triebe an die Steigdrähte im Frühjahr
Winding the young shoots around the wires in spring

Transport der geernteten Reben vom Hopfengarten zum Bauernhof
Transporting the harvested vines from the hop gardens to the farmyard

Einhängen der Reben in die Hopfenpflückmaschine
Hooking up the vines to the hop-picking machine

Ernte wie anno dazumal beim Hopfenzupfer-Jahrtag in Scheyern
Manual harvesting during the hop-picking anniversary in Scheyern

Das grüne Gold der Hallertau: frische geerntete Hopfendolden.
Hallertau's green gold: freshly harvested hop cones

Pfaffenhofen ist mit über 24 000 Einwohnern die größte Stadt der Hallertau, die sich von Hohenwart im Westen bis Rottenburg an der Laaber im Osten und von den Jurahöhen bei Altmannstein bis nach Süden ins Ampertal bei Moosburg erstreckt. Bekannt geworden ist die Region als größtes zusammenhängendes Hopfenanbaugebiet der Welt.

Rund 600 000 Zentner des „grünen Goldes“, wie man das zur Bierherstellung benötigte Doldengewächs auch bezeichnet, werden hier jedes Jahr auf einer Anbaufläche von rund 15 000 Hektar geerntet.

Ab Mitte Juni, wenn die Kletterpflanzen ihre Gerüsthöhe von sechs Metern erreicht haben, dominieren die sattgrünen Hopfengärten das Landschaftsbild in der Umgebung von Pfaffenhofen. Und nach der Ernte im September sind es die aus den Feldern ragenden kahlen Holzstangen, die dem Hügelland seinen ganz besonderen, unverwechselbaren Charakter geben.

Vom Anbinden der jungen Triebe an die Steigdrähte im Frühjahr bis zur Ernte im August und September bestimmt die mit dem Hanf verwandte Kulturpflanze den Tagesablauf der Landwirte. „Der Hopfen will jeden Tag seinen Herrn sehen“, sagt ein alter Holledauer Bauernspruch.

Bis Ende der 1950er Jahre war die Hopfenernte noch reine Handarbeit. An die 200 000 Saisonhelfer strömten alljährlich aus ganz Bayern und darüber hinaus in die Holledau. Heute wird die Ernte weitgehend maschinell erledigt. Die viel besungene Hopfenzupferromantik lebt nur noch bei Brauchtumsfesten auf, wo man die Dolden noch mit der Hand von den Reben zupfen kann.

With more than 24,000 inhabitants, Pfaffenhofen is the largest city in the Hallertau region, which stretches from Hohenwart in the west to Rottenburg an der Laaber in the east, and from the Jura heights near Altmannstein southwards to Ampertal near Moosburg. The region acquired its fame as the largest single hop-growing area in the world.

Every year, around 600,000 tons of the “green gold”, as the hop cones used in beer production are called, are harvested here on a crop area of about 15,000 hectares.

Starting in mid-June, when the hop vines reach the tops of the six-metre poles, the bright green hop plantations dominate the landscape around Pfaffenhofen. And after the harvest in September, it's the bare wooden poles sticking out of the fields that lend the hilly landscape its distinctive character.

From the moment when the young shoots are attached to the wires in spring until the cones are harvested in August and September, the hop farmers' daily routine is determined by this hemp-like crop plant. “A hop wants to see its master every day,” as Holledau farmers often say. Hop-harvesting was an entirely manual task until the end of the 1950s.

Up to 200,000 seasonal workers from all over Bavaria and beyond used to stream into the Holledau, whereas now the crop is harvested mostly by machines. These days, the popular idealized image of hop-picking lives on only at traditional festivals that celebrate old customs, where the hop cones can still be picked from the vine by hand.

Hopfenlandschaft bei Sulzbach, westlich von Pfaffenhofen.
Hop landscape near Sulzbach, west of Pfaffenhofen.

Affalterbach wird schon um 755 als „Affoltrapah" (Apfelbaumbach) urkundlich erwähnt. Der Turm der Pfarrkirche St. Michael stammt aus dem 14. Jahrhundert.
Affalterbach is mentioned in a document written as long ago as 755, where it appears as *Affoltrapah* ("apple tree stream"). The tower of the parish church of St Michael dates back to the 14th century.

6

PFAFFENHOFENER ORTSTEILE
PFAFFENHOFEN: ITS VARIOUS PARTS

Neben der alten Kernstadt gehören zum Mittelzentrum Pfaffenhofen noch zwölf ehemals selbstständige Gemeinden, die bei der Gebietsreform von 1971 bis 1978 eingemeindet wurden. Mit ihnen kamen über 60 Dörfer, Weiler und Einödhöfe zum Gebiet der Kreisstadt, das heute eine Fläche von 92 Quadratkilometern umschließt. 85 Prozent sind land- und forstwirtschaftlich genutzt. Von den rund 25 000 Stadtbürgern leben etwa ein Viertel in den Ortsteilen, die sich ihren ursprünglichen ländlichen Charakter noch weitgehend bewahrt haben.

Apart from the core of the old city itself, Pfaffenhofen includes 12 formerly independent municipalities that were incorporated into this regional centre during the municipal territory reform of 1971 to 1978. With them came more than 60 villages, hamlets and isolated farms that were also added to the territory of the district capital. That area now measures 92 square kilometres, of which 85 per cent is used agriculturally and for forestry purposes. About a quarter of the almost 25,000 inhabitants live in parts of the city or in villages that have largely preserved their original rural character.

Wahrzeichen des Ortsteils Förnbach ist die im 15. Jahrhundert erbaute Pfarrkirche Mariä Himmelfahrt (oben links).
Noch aus dem 13./14. Jahrhundert stammt der Turm der Pfarrkirche St. Sebastian in Uttenhofen. Das Langhaus wurde um 1905 neu errichtet (unten links).
Zu den ältesten Kirchen im Pfaffenhofener Umland gehört St. Peter im Weiler Griesbach bei Uttenhofen. Warum der spätromanische Backsteinbau mit dem wehrhaften Turm aus dem 12. Jahrhundert nie verputzt wurde, ist bis heute nicht geklärt (oben rechts).
Von den Hügeln über dem Ortsteil Kleinreichertshofen bietet sich ein herrlicher Blick nach Süden hinunter ins Ilmtal (Mitte rechts).
Zahlreiche alte Mühlen säumen die Ilmufer im Gebiet der Stadt Pfaffenhofen, wie die Zierlmühle an der nördlichen Gemeindegrenze (unten rechts).

Förnbach's landmark is the 15th-century parish church of the Assumption of the Virgin Mary (top left).
The tower of the parish church of St Sebastian in Uttenhofen dates from the 13th/14th century. The nave was rebuilt in 1905 (bottom left).
One of the oldest churches in the Pfaffenhofen environs is St Peter's in the hamlet of Griesbach, near Uttenhofen. Why the late Romanesque brick building with its 12th-century fortified tower was never plastered remains a mystery (top right).
From the hills above Kleinreichertshofen, there's a magnificent view to the south, all the way down into the Ilm valley (centre right).
There are many old mills scattered along the banks of the River Ilm in the area around Pfaffenhofen, such as this one at Zierlmühle, on the northern municipal boundary (bottom right).

Zeugnisse der Volksfrömmigkeit sind die vielen Kapellen, Bildstöcke und Feldkreuze, die dem Wanderer überall in der Umgebung der Kreisstadt begegnen. Von links: Kapelle im Ortsteil Eberstetten und Feldkreuz zwischen Förnbach und Uttenhofen; unten: Kapelle am Riedhof und Bildstock in Streitdorf.

The many chapels, wayside shrines and field crosses that hikers and ramblers encounter everywhere in the region bear witness to the piety of the local population. From the left: a chapel in Eberstetten and a field cross between Förnbach and Uttenhofen; below: a chapel at Riedhof and a wayside shrine in Streitdorf.

Gundamsried (oben links), schon um 1030 erstmals urkundlich erwähnt, wurde vermutlich von Columbanermönchen gegründet. Mit der um 1200 errichteten Kirche St. Germanus hat es sich bis heute seinen Charakter als idyllisches Bauerndorf bewahrt.
Gleiches gilt für Walkersbach, dessen Kirche dem heiligen Martin geweiht ist (oben rechts) und den am weitesten nördlich gelegenen Pfaffenhofener Ortsteil Eja mit der im Jahre 1874 errichteten Marienkapelle (Foto unten).

Gundamsried (top left), first mentioned in a document around 1030, was presumably founded by Columban monks. With the church of St Germanus, built around 1200, it has preserved its character as an idyllic farming village to this day.
The same goes for Walkersbach, whose church is dedicated to St Martin (top right), and Eja, Pfaffenhofen's northernmost village, with its Lady Chapel, built in 1874 (bottom).

Wahrzeichen von Haimpertshofen, seit dem 12. Jahrhundert als Adelssitz nachgewiesen, ist die Pfarrkirche St. Stephan (Foto links). Das im 15. Jahrhundert errichtete Gotteshaus besitzt eine künstlerisch bemerkenswerte Innenausstattung. Jedes Jahr am zweiten Weihnachtsfeiertag werden Reiter und Pferde beim traditionellen Stephaniritt rund um die Kirche gesegnet.

Die Verehrung der Muttergottes als Schutzpatronin Bayerns ist auch in unserer Gegend weit verbreitet. Davon zeugt diese Marienkapelle an einem Feldweg zwischen Angkofen und Gittenbach (rechts).

The landmark in Haimpertshofen, recorded as an aristocratic estate since the 12th century, is the parish church of St Stephan (photo left). The 15th-century church has an artistically remarkable interior. Every year on the second day of Christmas, riders and horses are blessed as they circle the church in the traditional *Stephaniritt.*

Veneration of Our Lady as the patron saint of Bavaria is widespread in our region, too, as testified by this Lady Chapel on a country lane between Angkofen and Gittenbach (right).

Tegernbach mit seiner Pfarrkirche St. Maria (Bild links) war einer der größten Orte, die bei der Gebietsreform in den 1970er Jahren nach Pfaffenhofen eingemeindet wurden.
Mit Tegernbach kamen auch mehrere Nachbardörfer zur Kreisstadt. Während das ländliche Ortsbild von Eutenhofen (oben rechts) kaum von modernen Einflüssen gestört wird, zeigt sich in Ehrenberg (unten rechts) schon der unschöne Preis, den unsere Dörfer und die Landschaft für die Energiewende bezahlen müssen: Statt roter Ziegeldächer, die über Jahrhunderte das Ortsbild prägten, ist die Pfarrkirche St. Ulrich heute von Solarmodulen eingerahmt.

Together with its parish church of St Maria (photo left), Tegernbach was one of the largest places to be incorporated into Pfaffenhofen during the municipal territory reform of the 1970s.
With Tegernbach came several neighbouring villages. Whereas Eutenhofen's outward rural appearance (top right) has hardly been marred by modern influences, Ehrenberg (bottom right) is already displaying the unsightly price our villages and countryside are having to pay for the turnaround in the country's energy policy: instead of the red tiled roofs that for centuries characterized the look of a place, the parish church of St Ulrich is today framed by solar panels.

Im idyllisch gelegenen Göbelsbach, 1998 beim Wettbewerb „Unser Dorf soll schöner werden" zum Landessieger gekürt, steht der 150 Jahre alte „Troobartl"-Hof (oben). Die Malerin Doris Prütting und ihr Ehemann Lorenz haben das Anwesen liebevoll restauriert und veranstalten hier alljährlich im Sommer ein großes Kunstfest.
Hoch auf den Hügeln südlich von Göbelsbach liegt inmitten von saftigen Wiesen und fruchtbaren Feldern das malerische Dorf Menzenbach (unten).

Göbelsbach is an idyllic setting for the 150-year-old Troobartl farm (top). In 1988, Göbelsbach was declared the winner of the state competition "Beautify our Village".
The artist Doris Prütting and her husband, Lorenz, have lovingly restored the property and organize a big art festival here every summer.
High on the hills south of Göbelsbach, in the midst of lush meadows and fertile fields, lies the picturesque village of Menzenbach (bottom).

60 Meter hoch ist der Antennenmast der TV- und Radio-Sendeanlage
olfsberg, der den ganzen südlichen Landkreis Pfaffenhofen überragt
roßes Foto rechts).
m Rand des Waldweges zwischen Menzenbach und Vieth begegnet man
nheimlichen Zeugnissen der Volksfrömmigkeit: Totenbretter, die an ver-
orbene Angehörige erinnern (Foto oben links).
der Nachbarschaft finden sich zahlreiche idyllische Bauerndörfer, wie
ienhöfe (oben), sowie die Weiler Fürholzen (unten links) und Schabenberg.

The antenna mast of the Wolfsberg TV and radio transmitter towers 160 metres above the entire southern part of the Pfaffenhofen administrative district (large photo, right).
On the edge of the forest track between Menzenbach and Vieth, one finds eerie evidence of local piety: Totenbretter, wooden boards commemorating deceased relatives (top left).
There are numerous idyllic farming villages in the neighbourhood, such as Kienhöfe (top), the hamlet Fürholzen (bottom left) and Schabenberg.

Blick auf Niederscheyern im Herbst. Durch neue Baugebiete ist der Pfaffenhofener Ortsteil seit der Eingemeindung 1978 sehr stark gewachsen. Die Pfarrkirche Mariä Himmelfahrt war im 17. und 18. Jahrhundert Ziel einer bedeutenden Wallfahrt. In den Mirakelbüchern finden sich zahlreiche Aufzeichnungen zu Gebetserhörungen und geopferte Votivgaben aus der Wachszieherei in Pfaffenhofen (Foto unten)
Der Doderhof bei Sulzbach (oben rechts) und das Höfelmaier-Anwesen bei Niederscheyern sind zwei typische Einödhöfe, wie man sie in der Umgebung der Kreisstadt vielfach antrifft.

View of Niederscheyern in autumn. Since its incorporation into Pfaffenhofen in 1978, this locality has grown considerably through the addition of new land-use areas. The parish church of the Assumption of the Virgin Mary was an important place of pilgrimage in the 17th and 18th centuries. In the books of miracles, there are many recorded instances of prayers that have been answered and votive offerings from the candlemaking workshop in Pfaffenhofen (bottom photo).
The Doderhof near Sulzbach (top right) and the Höfelmaier property near Niederscheyern are typical of the isolated farms that one often finds in the areas surrounding the district capital.

Erinnerungen an die Toskana weckt diese Aufnahme von einem abgeernteten Getreidefeld bei Haimpertshofen.
This photo of a harvested wheat field near Haimpertshofen evokes memories of Tuscany.

7 SEHENSWERTER LANDKREIS

A REGION THAT'S WORTH SEEING

Der Landkreis Pfaffenhofen ist reich an Sehenswürdigkeiten, kulturellen Attraktionen und landschaftlichen Reizen. Eines der beliebtesten Ausflugsziele und auch der geschichtlich bedeutsamste Ort in der Umgebung der Kreisstadt ist Scheyern, die Wiege des bayerischen Herrschergeschlechtes der Wittelsbacher. Die Grafen von Scheyern waren im Jahre 1106 nach Oberwittelsbach bei Aichach umgezogen und hatten ihre Stammburg dem Benediktinerorden übergeben, der hier seit 1119 ansässig ist. In der Fürstengruft der Basilika sind mehrere Wittelsbacher Herzöge beigesetzt. Wertvollster Schatz der Abtei ist die Heiligkreuz-Reliquie, ein Holzsplitter vom Kreuz Christi. Auf dem Benediktus-Wanderweg bei den idyllischen Klosterweihern kann man auf den Spuren von Joseph Ratzinger wandeln, der hier als Kardinal vor seiner Wahl zum Papst des Öfteren Urlaub gemacht hatte. Und nach der Wanderung lockt der Biergarten mit Spezialitäten der bayerischen Küche und kühlen Getränken aus der eigenen Klosterbrauerei zur gemütlichen Einkehr.

The Pfaffenhofen district has a wealth of interesting places, cultural highlights and scenic attractions. One of the best-loved excursion destinations and a historically significant location around Pfaffenhofen is Scheyern, the cradle of Bavaria's Wittelsbach ruling dynasty. The Scheyer dukes had left their family seat in 1106 to move to Oberwittelsbach near Aichach, handing over their ancestral castle to the Benedictine order, which has been based here since 1119. A number of Wittelsbach dukes are interred in the basilica's royal crypt. The most precious treasure at the abbey is the relic of the Holy Cross, a splinter of wood from the Cross of Christ. On the Benedictus hiking trail near the idyllic monastery ponds, one can walk in the footsteps of Joseph Ratzinger, who used to holiday here when he was a cardinal and before he was elected Pope. And after taking a walk, there's the promise of a relaxing rest in the beer garden with its Bavarian culinary specialities and cool drinks from the monastery's own brewery.

Die um das Jahr 1210 errichtete romanische Basilika St. Arsatius ist das Wahrzeichen der Gemeinde Ilmmünster (Bild oben links). Die Kirche beherbergt eine Reihe bedeutender Kunstschätze, darunter den Sarkophag mit den Reliquien des heiligen Arsatius.

In Sichtweite zu Ilmmünster liegt auf einem Hügel die 1599 erbaute Wallfahrtskirche Herrnrast (links unten).

Das mittelalterliche Wasserschloss bildet die malerische Kulisse für die Golfer in Reichertshausen (unten rechts).

Das in seinen Ursprüngen aus der Spätgotik um 1500 stammende Hochschloss der Freiherrn von Freyberg ist neben der Pfarrkirche St. Johannes das Wahrzeichen der Gemeinde Jetzendorf (oben rechts).

The Romanesque basilica of St Arsatius, built circa 1210, is the landmark of the parish of Ilmmünster (top left). The church houses a series of important art treasures, including the sarcophagus containing Arsatius's holy relics.

Within view of Ilmmünster and situated on a hill is the pilgrimage church of Herrnrast, built in 1599. (bottom left).

The medieval moated castle in Reichertshausen provides a picturesque setting for the golfers on the green (bottom right).

In its origins, the high castle of the barons von Freyberg dates from the late Gothic period around 1500. Along with the parish church of St Johannes, it's a landmark of the Jetzendorf parish (top right).

Gasthaus zum alten

Bilder Seite 128:
Die alte Pfarrkirche St. Johannes und das Gasthaus Alter Wirt bilden mit dem Schloss ein historisches Ensemble im Rohrbacher Ortszentrum (kleines Bild oben).
Das Deutsche Hopfenmuseum in Wolnzach (oben rechts) ist die weltweit größte Sammlung zur Geschichte des Hopfenanbaus. Mit rund 20 000 Besuchern pro Jahr zählt das Museum zu den wichtigsten touristischen Anziehungspunkten im Landkreis Pfaffenhofen.
Die zwischen Rohrbach und Langenbruck gelegene Kirche St. Kastulus, einst ein berühmter Hallertauer Wallfahrtsort, ist auch heute noch ein beliebtes Ausflugsziel (unten links).
In dem hoch über dem Paartal gelegenen ehemaligen Benediktinerinnenkloster Hohenwart ist heute ein Behindertenzentrum von Regens Wagner ansässig (unten rechts).

Bilder Seite 129:
Der Spargelanbau breitet sich im Landkreis immer weiter aus. Ein Zentrum des Edelgemüses ist neben Hohenwart die Gemeinde Pörnbach (oben links).
Der Geisenfelder Stadtplatz zählt zu den schönsten historischen Ortszentren im Landkreis (rechts).
Das um 1220 erbaute Kirchlein von Ainau bei Geisenfeld ist ein herausragendes Denkmal der romanischen Baukunst im Landkreis (unten links).

Photos on page 128:
The old parish church of St Johannes, the Alter Wirt tavern and the castle form a historic ensemble in the centre of Rohrbach (small photo, top).
The German Hop Museum in Wolnzach (top right) is the world's largest special collection of exhibits on the history of hop-growing. It attracts some 20,000 visitors every year, making it one of the biggest tourist magnets in the district.
Situated between Rohrbach and Langenbruck, the St Kastulus church, once a famous place of pilgrimage in the Hallertau region, is today still a popular excursion destination (bottom left).
Set high above the Paar valley, the former Benedictine convent Hohenwart is today a centre for disabled people, belonging to the Regens Wagner Foundation (bottom right).

Photos on page 129:
Asparagus cultivation is spreading in the Pfaffenhofen district. One of the centres for growing this delicacy, alongside Hohenwart, is Pörnbach (top left).
The town square in Geisenfeld ranks as one of the loveliest town centres in the Pfaffenhofen district (right).
The little church in Ainau, near Geisenfeld, dates from circa 1220 and is an outstanding monument to Romanesque architecture in the district (bottom left).

Manching war schon in vorchristlicher Zeit ein kulturelles Zentrum von überregionaler Bedeutung. Die Geschichte des Ortes ist im Kelten- und Römermuseum dokumentiert (links oben).
Die nahe gelegenen Kiesweiher im Feilenmoos sind ein beliebtes Erholungszentrum der Landkreisbewohner (rechts).

Eine Bronzestatue erinnert vor der Burgmauer in Vohburg an die tragische Liebesgeschichte zwischen dem Bayernherzog Albrecht und der Baderstochter Agnes Bernauer (unten).

Even in pre-Christian times, Manching was already an important cultural centre that was well known outside the region. The history of Manching is documented in the local Celtic-Roman Museum (top left).
The nearby gravel ponds in Feilenmoos are a popular recreational centre for people living in the district (right).

A bronze statue in front of the castle wall in Vohburg reminds us of the tragic love story between the Bavarian Duke Albrecht III and Agnes Bernauer, the daughter of a barber (bottom).

Hallertauer Frühling im Schweitenkirchener Hügelland.
Springtime in the hilly landscape of Schweitenkirchen in the Hallertau region.

Zu den Autoren:

WILLY HAILER, 1949 in Pfaffenhofen geboren, war fast 40 Jahre (bis 2010) Redaktionsleiter des Pfaffenhofener Kurier. Neben seiner journalistischen Arbeit für die Lokalzeitung veröffentlichte er zahlreiche Texte und Fotos in Zeitschriften, Broschüren und Büchern wie „Auf den Spuren des grünen Goldes", „Unser Landkreis Pfaffenhofen" und „Geheimnisvolle Plätze in der Hallertau" (Text: Reinhard Haiplik). Willy Hailer arbeitet heute als freier Journalist in Pfaffenhofen.

ANTON RITZER, geboren 1947 in Passau, kam 1970 als Polizeibeamter nach Pfaffenhofen. Seit 1972 ist er Mitglied der vhs-Fotofreunde, die er über drei Jahrzehnte als 1. und 2. Vorsitzender führte. Zu seinen größten Erfolgen als Fotograf gehören der 2. Preis beim weltweit für Profis und Amateure ausgeschriebenen Mazda-Wettbewerb 1990, eine Goldmedaille und Platz 4 in der Gesamtwertung der Bundesfotoschau 2008 sowie Spitzenplatzierungen bei Bayerischen und Oberbayerischen Meisterschaften. Ritzers Bilder wurden in zahlreichen Zeitungen, Zeitschriften und Büchern veröffentlicht und sind regelmäßig in Ausstellungen zu sehen.

IMPRESSUM

Herausgeber und Verlag
Galli Verlag + Vertrieb GmbH, 86558 Hohenwart
Text, Konzeption und Redaktion
Willy Hailer, 85262 Pfaffenhofen
Fotos
Willy Hailer, Anton Ritzer, Stadtarchiv Pfaffenhofen und andere Autoren (siehe Bildnachweis).
Gestaltung, Layout und Prepress
two8 grafikdesign, 80469 München, www.two8.de
Übersetzung
Danko Szabó
Gesamtherstellung
Galli Verlag + Vertrieb GmbH
Am Steinberg 1, 86558 Hohenwart
Telefon: 08443 8916, Telefax: 08443 8917
galli-verlag@t-online.de
www.galli-verlag.de

Bildnachweis:
ADV, Archäologische Dienstleistungen, Neuburg: Seite 9, rechts;
Eble Joachim, Architektur/Atelier Dreiseitl/moka-studio: S. 100, unten rechts.;
Daiichi Sankyo; S. 112, 113;
Denalane Joy: S. 89, rechts;
Galli Josef: 128 o. r.;
Gerrard Alexandra: 83 o. l.; 87 o. l.;
Hailer Willy: Seite 5 oben, 2. von oben, 3. v. o.; 6 o .r.; S. 8; 11; 13; 15; 16 o.; 17; 19; 21 u.; 22; 23; 26 u.; 30; 31; 34; 37; 41 o. r.; 43; 44 r.; 45 r.; 46 r.; 47; 48 r.; 49 l; 51 o. l.; 52 u. l.; 53 r.; 54; 55; 56; 57; 58 o., m., u. r.; 59; 60; 61; 62; 63; 64; 66; 67 l.; 69; 72 o.; 73 o.; 74 l., m., 76; 81 o. l; m. l.; u. r.; 86 o. l., m. l.; 88 u. l.; 89 o. l.; 90 u. l.; 91 u. l.; 92 u. r.; 93 l., o. r.; 94 u.; 95; 97 r.; 99 o. r., u. l.; 100 u. l.; 101 l.; 102; 103 o., u. r.; 105 o. r.; 106 o. r., u.; 108 o. r.; 109 o. l.; 111 o.; 114; 115; 116; 117 o. l., o. r., m. r.; 118; 120; 121 r.; 122 o.; 123 o. r., u. l., u. r.; 124 o. l.; 126; 127; 128 o. l., 128 u.; 129; 130; 131.
Hippwerk: S. 110; 111u.;
hutterreimann Landschaftsarchitektur, Berlin: 103 u. l.;
Iwanowski Sarah: S. 89, 2. v. l.;
Pfaffenhofener Kurier: *Eibisch Manfred*, S. 21 o. l.; *Kraus Michael*: S. 9, links; 21 o. r.;
Privat: *Hipp Nikolaus*: S. 91, o. r.; *Hipp Hans:* S. 93, m. r.; *Hipp Josef:* S. 90, o.;
Reitmeier Max: S. 91, o. l.;
Ritzer Anton: Titelseite; Seiten: 5 u.; 6 l.; 7; 12; 25; 26 o.; 27; 29; 32; 33; 40; 41 l., u. r.; 42; 44 l.; 45 l.; 46 l.; 48 l.; 49 r.; 50; 51 o. r., u. l.; 52 o. l.; u. r.; 53 l.; 58 l. u.; 65; 67 r.; 68; 70; 71; 72 u.; 73 u.; 74 r.; 75; 77; 79; 80; 81 o. r., u. l.; u. m.; 82; 83 o. r.; 85; 87 u.; 88 o. l., o. r.; 90 u. r.; 92 l. o.; 94 o. l., o. r.; 96 l.; 97 l., m.; 98; 99 o. l., u. r.; 101 r.; 104; 105 o. l., o. m., u.; 106 o. l., o. m.; 107; 108 o. l., u.; 109 o. r.; u. l.; 117 u. l., u. r.; 119; 121 l.; 122 u.; 123 r., o. l.; 124 o. r., u.; 125;
Stadt Pfaffenhofen: 87 o. r.; 96 r.; *Steinbüchler Elisabeth:* S. 78 o.; 86 u. l.;
Wagner Hanns: S. 16, u.;
Wilfling Michael: S. 89, 3. v. l.

Das Werk einschließlich aller seiner Teile ist in der Gesamtheit urheberrechtlich geschützt. Jede Verwertung ist ohne Zustimmung des Herausgebers unzulässig. Das gilt insbesondere für Vervielfältigungen, Mikroverfilmungen, Übersetzungen und die Einspeicherung und Verarbeitung in elektronischen Systemen. Auszüge und Veröffentlichungen aus diesem Objekt nur mit Genehmigung des Herausgebers.

Änderungen und Irrtum vorbehalten.

Printed in Germany 2012

About the authors:

WILLY HAILER was born in Pfaffenhofen in 1949. For almost 40 years (until 2010) he was chief editor of the *Pfaffenhofener Kurier*. In addition to his journalistic work for this local newspaper he also published numerous texts and photos in magazines, brochures and books, including *Auf den Spuren des grünen Goldes, Unser Landkreis Pfaffenhofen* and *Geheimnisvolle Plätze in der Hallertau* (Text: Reinhard Haiplik). Willy Hailer is a freelance journalist in Pfaffenhofen.

ANTON RITZER was born in Passau in 1947. He cam to Pfaffenhofen in 1970 as a police officer. He ha been a member of vhs-Fotofreunde since 1972 an served as its chairman and deputy chairman fo more than three decades. Among his greatest suc cesses as a photographer are the 2nd prize he wo in the 1990 worldwide Mazda competition for pro fessionals and amateurs, a gold medal and overa 4th place at the 2008 *Bundesfotoschau*, along wit top rankings at Bavarian and Upper Bavarian cham pionships. Ritzer's pictures have been published i numerous newspapers, magazines and books, an are regularly on show at exhibitions.

IMPRESSUM

Publisher
Galli Verlag + Vertrieb GmbH, 86558 Hohenwart
Author and Editor
Willy Hailer, 85262 Pfaffenhofen
Photos
Anton Ritzer, Willy Hailer and the town archives of Pfaffenhofen a. d. Ilm
Design, Layout and Prepress
two8 grafikdesign, 80469 Munich, www.two8.de
Translation
Danko Szabó
Overall Production
Galli Verlag + Vertrieb GmbH
Am Steinberg 1, 86558 Hohenwart
Phone: +49-8443 8916, Fax: +49-8443 8917
galli-verlag@t-online.de
www.galli-verlag.de

Photo credits:
ADV, Archäologische Dienstleistungen, Neuburg: Seite 9, rechts;
Eble Joachim, Architektur/Atelier Dreiseitl/moka-studio: S. 100, unten rechts.;
Daiichi Sankyo; S. 112, 113;
Denalane Joy: S. 89, rechts;
Galli Josef: 128 o. r.;
Gerrard Alexandra: 83 o. l.; 87 o. l.;
Hailer Willy: Seite 5 oben, 2. von oben, 3. v. o.; 6 o .r.; S. 8; 11; 13; 15; 16 o.; 17; 19; 21 u.; 22; 23; 26 u.; 30; 31; 34; 37; 41 r.; 43; 44 r.; 45 r.; 46 r.; 47; 48 r.; 49 l; 51 o. l.; 52 u. 53 r.; 54; 55; 56; 57; 58 o., m., u. r.; 59; 60; 61; 62; 6 64; 66; 67 l.; 69; 72 o.; 73 o.; 74 l., m., 76; 81 o. l; m. u. r.; 86 o. l., m. l.; 88 u. l.; 89 o. l.; 90 u. l.; 91 u. l.; 92 r.; 93 l., o. r.; 94 u.; 95; 97 r.; 99 o. r., u. l.; 100 u. l.; 10 l.; 102; 103 o., u. r.; 105 o. r.; 106 o. r., u.; 108 o. r.; 10 o. l.; 111 o.; 114; 115; 116; 117 o. l., o. r., m. r.; 11 120; 121 r.; 122 o.; 123 o. r., u. l., u. r.; 124 o. l.; 12 127; 128 o. l., 128 u.; 129; 130; 131.
Hippwerk: S. 110; 111u.;
hutterreimann Landschaftsarchitektur, Berlin: 103 u.
Iwanowski Sarah: S. 89, 2. v. l.;
Pfaffenhofener Kurier: *Eibisch Manfred*, S. 21 o. *Kraus Michael*: S. 9, links; 21 o. r.;
Privat: *Hipp Nikolaus*: S. 91, o. r.; *Hipp Hans:* S. 9 m. r.; *Hipp Josef:* S. 90, o.;
Reitmeier Max: S. 91, o. l.;
Ritzer Anton: Titelseite; Seiten: 5 u.; 6 l.; 7; 12; 25; o.; 27; 29; 32; 33; 40; 41 l., u. r.; 42; 44 l.; 45 l.; 46 l.; l.; 49 r.; 50; 51 o. r., u. l.; 52 o. l.; u. r.; 53 l.; 58 l. u.; 6 67 r.; 68; 70; 71; 72 u.; 73 u.; 74 r.; 75; 77; 79; 80; o. r., u. l.; u. m.; 82; 83 o. r.; 85; 87 u.; 88 o. l., o. r.; u. r.; 92 l. o.; 94 o. l., o. r.; 96 l.; 97 l., m.; 98; 99 o. l., r.; 101 r.; 104; 105 o. l., o. m., u.; 106 o. l., o. m.; 10 108 o. l., u.; 109 o. r.; u. l.; 117 u. l., u. r.; 119; 121 122 u.; 123 r., o. l.; 124 o. r., u.; 125;
Stadt Pfaffenhofen: 87 o. r.; 96 r.; *Steinbüchler Elis beth:* S. 78 o.; 86 u. l.;
Wagner Hanns: S. 16, u.;
Wilfling Michael: S. 89, 3. v. l;

This publication, including all its texts, is protected by copyright. No part of this book may be used without the consent of the publisher. This applies in particular to duplication, microfilming, translatio storage on databases and reworking in electronic systems. Permission must be obtained from the cop right owner if you wish to publish extracts from this work.

Subject to changes and corrections.

Printed in Germany, 2012